Royal DisClosure

Royal DisClosure

Problematics of Representation
In French Classical Tragedy

by

Harriet Stone

SUMMA PUBLICATIONS, INC.
Birmingham, Alabama
1987

327446

for my parents

Portions of the present study first appeared, in very different form, in the following journals. I thank the journals for permission to reprint this material:

"A Tightening of Rhetorical Conventions in *Le Cid, Horace, Cinna,* and *Polyeucte,*" *Theatre Journal* 34 (Oct. 1982), pp. 302-21.

"Heroic Imperatives and Psychic Mechanisms in Corneille's *Rodogune, Héraclius,* and *Œdipe,*" *Essays in Literature* 10 (Fall 1983), pp. 283-98.

"The Tragedy of Andromaque's Sacrifice" *Romanic Review* LXXV, 4 (Nov. 1984), pp. 424-31.

"The Seduction of the Father in *Phèdre* and *Athalie,*" in *Actes de Baton Rouge,* Selma A. Zebouni, ed. (Paris: Biblio 17, 1986), pp. 153-64.

Acknowledgments

Work on a project such as this begins long before the first word is ever put on paper and continues each day after the solitary sessions at the desk are complete. I should like to thank the many friends, colleagues, and teachers who have seen me through its vicissitudes, with special thanks to those whose relation encompasses all three roles.

I am grateful to Al Cook, whose example and counsel supported the early stages of the manuscript, and to Jimmy Jones, from whose encouragement and kind reading of a later draft I profited. I especially want to acknowledge the efforts made by Jack Grigsby to assist in the publication of this work.

I should like to thank as well Pascal Ifri, Emma Kafelanos, Joseph Loewenstein, Naomi Schor, Michael Sherberg, Lynne Tatlock, Arnold Weinstein, Janet Whatley, and Colette Winn for reading all or portions of the manuscript. Thanks are likewise due to the anonymous readers of the manuscript. Julie Bell, Andy Blocha, Mark Farber, and Nuri Farber are to be commended for their patient assistance with the computer. I am most appreciative of the efforts made by William Carter in bringing this work to publication, as of the excellent copy editing achieved by Lynn Carter.

I wish also to acknowledge the support of Washington University, whose generous assistance has enabled the book to enter its final phase.

Contents

Introduction

Re-presentation: A Mirrored Difference

> Vous dites dans la seconde (objection),
> que *la vérité des axiomes qui se font*
> *recevoir clairement et distinctement à*
> *notre esprit est manifeste par elle-même.*
> Je l'accorde aussi pour tout le temps
> qu'ils sont clairement et distinctement
> compris, parce que notre âme est de
> telle nature, qu'elle ne peut pas refuser
> de se rendre à ce qu'elle comprend
> distinctement....
>
> Descartes, *Lettre à Regius*

REPRESENTATION, IN THE MOST GENERAL SENSE, is a likeness. It refers to literature's imitation of some reality outside of itself (mimesis). The present study proposes to represent French classical representations of tragedy. It will focus on representation as a dramatic praxis: re-presentation. To re-present is to present again, to present something other. The book means to establish re-presentation as a model for reading not only the patriarchal historiography of Corneille and Racine but the (other) history that their tragedies (conspicuously) conceal.

Specifically, the term re-presentation is intended to join the concepts of imitation and repetition. Re-presentation suggests that tragedy's imitation of an external referent is grounded in the functioning of doubled forms: juxtapositions, substitutions, ritual cycles, play of past and present, presence and absence. The point of what follows is not, however, to show that this activity results in the objectification of a given model, to authenticate in this way the power of the patriarchy. On the contrary, re-presentation implies that the process of objectification remains incomplete. Though it extends the notion of mimesis from the image of a world centered in the role of the prince to the analogic chain responsible for creating this image, re-presentation paradoxically exposes the limits of intellectual systems which order knowledge through resemblances. The re-presentations of tragedy ordered through the chapters of this book—a cycle that includes the tragedies of Corneille and Racine, philosophical texts of the classical period, and modern literary theory—will look beyond the reproduction of a unique paradigm of patriarchal power to the tragic loss of alterity that this paradigm and this power impose.

Tragedy contains within itself the potential to represent something other than history as a fixed image or point of view. Although Corneille and Racine both legitimate a particular *doxa*, or perceived ideology, through imitation, they re-present imitation as the process through which truth redoubles truth. If the plays' mirrored forms affirm the pride and power of the monarchy, these forms are doubled so as to foil the identification process realized through imitation. The text's self-conscious references to its own activity suggest that the final power of representation is not to describe or to perfect an existing model but to create something for which no model exists. Consequently, knowledge is posited not as an act of cognition but as a process of reception that subverts some of the objective structures which order information.

In the tragedies of Corneille and Racine an objective view of reality is coordinated through forms whose recurrence establishes the continued power of the king—the hierarchical command that extends along a single line of vision from God to prince, to father, and to son. Yet this paradigm is unable to explain much of the play's action and its intrigue for the reader/spectator. The multiplication of a single, privileged point of view often fails, for example, to account adequately for the women's presence. Corneille's and Racine's heroines frequently challenge the conventions through which the play establishes society's beliefs as facts. Re-presentation imposes, beyond metaphorical closure, a difference within representation. John Lyons and Stephen Nichols attribute this difference to the polar concepts of mimesis: the fixing of an image of objective reality in the mind of the viewer, the indication of how the world is really; and the demonstration of the performative role of the artist and viewer, speaker and reader, as these determine reality as an idea, a subjective experience of the world.[1] Representation has come to mean both the objectification of knowledge and its opposite, the resistance to identities. Since Foucault's monumental work, we understand this resistance to result from the reader/spectator's questioning of "how the sheer fact of reproducing the world as a sign, the world as language, may expose and call into question precisely those conventions meant to systematize and objectify representation."[2] Following Foucault's analysis of the representation of representation, we no longer look to perceive identities simply. We also observe dissimilarity, the disappearance of the persons and events that constitute the subjects of mimesis, their resistance to identities assigned by such cognitive sciences as history and literary criticism.[3] It is for this reason that we can now discover in the concept of representation an explanation for our reception of the drama, our response to its performance. The observation of textual incongruities and of the indefinite status of events and characters is the consistent departure point for the readings of the classical texts included in this study.

Unmasking and remasking the dramatist's art, re-presentation is the theater within the theater of itself, the play of presence and absence. And we, not the characters who perform, are the ultimate beneficiaries of its versatile reflections. A character unable to achieve power within the political hierarchy is able to represent his power to us. Or, more precisely, a character denied status by the other characters in the drama is able to achieve status with us through the act of representing himself. Louis Marin theorizes that representation is the power to make present an absence. This re-presentation, he argues, implies the power to experience power.[4] While some characters in tragedy represent real authority, others who are denied this power create, as a consequence of their presence, the same power effect. Referring to the dictionary definition of representation as the exhibition of a title or right, Marin emphasizes the subject's capacity to make himself the center of the world whose authorization he seeks:

> Ainsi, par la représentation de son passeport à la frontière, non seulement son détenteur s'y présente réellement mais il présente sa présence légitime par le signe ou le titre qui autorise ou permet, voire contraint, sa présence. La représentation reste ici dans l'élément du même qu'elle intensifie par redoublement. En ce sens, elle est sa réflexion et représenter sera toujours se présenter représentant quelque chose.[5]

The same intensification is apparent in the texts of Corneille and Racine. Horace legitimates his own presence in Rome by presenting his dead enemy. Specifically, his re-presentation of this victory once Camille is dead—the narrative that constitutes his defense—allows him to appropriate power. Phèdre's account of her fantasy to Hippolyte similarly authenticates her desire because, consistent with Marin's analysis, "everything happens as if there were no world, no reality, except for and by a subject, center of this world."[6] In this depiction of the images that play in her mind, Phèdre makes Hippolyte feel the effects of her seduction. The problematics of representation, however, are evident in the fact that tragedy sanctions Horace while it condemns Phèdre. Horace survives as a hero the ordeal of his sister's murder; he is accorded a final honor. Phèdre must assume the guilt of her seduction. In terms of actual power, therefore, the two characters are diametrically opposed. Both Horace and Phèdre, however, constitute themselves as creating subjects within representation. Phèdre cannot really have Hippolyte's love, but she takes pleasure in this love as a consequence of her performance. Like Horace, she denies the mimetic completeness of the Law that excludes her.[7]

The case of Andromaque is more complex. Pyrrhus cannot be persuaded to abandon his love for Andromaque; she remains his captive. Yet Andromaque's justification of her position makes it impossible for us to consider this history an adequate description of the enacted drama. Believing that to love Pyrrhus is to sacrifice her love for Hector, Andromaque refuses to marry and faces Pyrrhus's threats as a suicide, as part of the same sacrifice. Andromaque's role prevents mimetic harmony in its doubling of capture with a promise—the assurance of fidelity which for the heroine is an exercise of freedom. Like Horace and Phèdre, therefore, Andromaque "presents herself representing something" that stabilizes the influences of the play which conspire against her, which refuse her presence.

Re-presentation allows for a concentration of power relations within the text while explaining the dispersive effects of this power for the reader/spectator.[8] Every tragedy has a mechanism for determining a subjective view of the world that contradicts the truth value implied by the objective imitation of patriarchal history. Chimène imitates Rodrigue; Camille challenges Horace; Cléopâtre's divisiveness threatens a natural reproduction; Eriphile is exchanged for Iphigénie; Athalie substitutes her own vision for that of the Jews, etc. Because it presumes a receiver, representation balances political power with perception, from *perspicare*, to see clearly. The characters cannot alter historical fact. They can, though, influence the ways in which this history is perceived by other characters and by us. They can and do complicate representation so that it is no longer explainable in terms of any single paradigm, however monolithic.

Rather than look to identify a particular referent or to specify the source of political control within the drama as so many examples of objective knowledge identified by representation, the readings which follow will develop a concept of knowledge that instead derives from the awareness that tragedy generates and legitimates internal questioning.[9] To re-present the history of a character's defeat is to recall as well the past as a pre-sacrificial or non-diminutive presence. The present loss, or absence, is continually juxtaposed in these dramas with the past absence-as-presence. Dramatic performance therefore requires that we construct a whole that is more than the sum of its parts. Symmetrical, proportionate, and infinitely re-presentable, French classical tragedy does establish a single sphere of influence. Yet if it is true that tragedy's recurrent forms represent an infinite return or an inexhaustible production of signifiers, it is likewise true that such constructs in turn imply, by their very predictability, certain restrictions upon knowledge. Corneille and Racine discover in ritual enactment the source not only of tragedy, a form perfected in its fullness, but of the tragic, a dimension of the real. The former suggests an unlimited potential, a boundless discourse, while the latter correlates specifically with the loss of difference that results from the duplication of forms within the drama. Corneille's and Racine's representations of tragedy will be shown to locate loss in the very mimetic process which sets in place the power structure conceived to protect against such loss.

Tracing how the enclosed space of the theater develops into a cycle, this cycle into a sacrificial rite, this rite into a narrative history, and this history into art, the readings which follow establish this book's own representational cycle. Coordinant with tragedy's various stages, the methodological framework shifts from chapter to chapter to show a broad range of interdisciplinary theory. From structuralism to theories of restorative violence and abjection that reflect the teachings of psycho-analysis, to studies of verisimilitude, the book's critical cycle moves in its last stage to Orientalism. While the latter term derives from a particular thematic interest in Racine's plays, it suggests the ways in which the classical texts orient the reader/spectator away from historical referents and into the play's own structures, away from conventions that make possible patriarchal history and towards the open space of confrontation, the invalidation of the same history. The book's second series of representations, that of the critical intertexts, parallels the production of meaning in the plays themselves. One of the underlying assumptions of the present investigation is that critical theory, like tragedy, imposes a view of reality, that all discourse forms the objects of which it speaks.[10] It shall be argued that critical methods also affect the tragic and that the knowledge structured through critical discourse is similarly modified (implicitly or explicitly) through the systematic application (re-presentation) of different critical models. This book intends then to consider the epistemological consequences of tragedy for the modern reader whose perception is a forward look back—for knowledge formed through both classical and contemporary critical practice. Locating meaning beyond resemblances—in the space of repetition rather than in these forms themselves—the present study means to understand the limits of the (very Western) mimetic model. The confluence of theatrical and critical discourses in a single cycle of representation shall discover meaning in textual activity that is inconsistent and dissimilar.[11]

The Cornelian hero creates for himself a world, while the Racinian hero creates chaos within a world already known to him. Yet this idea, in its suggestion of a contrast between order and disorder, is deceptive because both playwrights represent tragedy as the defeat of desire in the face of absolutism (the Father, Prince, Priest, and the destiny that unites them). Posited as an ineluctable but inevitable choice, desire is the individual's struggle for identity in a world that demands his subjugation to the will of society and the gods. The initial chapter on Corneille studies this repression in terms of a structural displacement which maps the path of the hero's deferred desire. Examining the concept of closure, readings of *Le Cid*, *Horace, Cinna*, and *Polyeucte* will detail how the successive stages of the hero's mastery are inversely related to a power structure that grows ever larger around him. Analyzing the hero's struggles to know and control other, self, country, and God, respectively, these four plays situate the hero within an ever-expanding political space that eludes his grasp. The hero, whose identity depends on his recognition of a geometrically perfect universe of infinite proportions, actually remains a figure without autonomy, forever equidistant from himself.

Extending the circle to the cycle of ritual enactment, the next two chapters study Corneille's and Racine's depictions of sacrificial violence.

The concept of heroism is shown to be inextricably linked to that of the *pharmakos*, or sacrificial victim. Interestingly, the theater's celebration assumes the sacred function of ritual while condemning ritual's own violence as profane. René Girard's extensive theorizing on this subject in *La Violence et le sacré* and *Des Choses cachées depuis la fondation du monde* provides a model for the structure of tragedy.[12] But where Girard posits an end to violence through the sacred, tragedy precludes sublimation by turning our attention back from an ethical ideal (the benevolence of the monarchy) towards the primitive state (desire) that it would refine. Both Corneille's middle plays (*Rodogune, Héraclius, and Œdipe*) and Racine's mythic plays (*Andromaque, Iphigénie, and Phèdre*) progress towards an open confrontation of incest and parricide. The question is not, finally, whether Girard's model is applicable to the tragedies of Corneille and Racine but whether the model can work a second time. The multiple re-presentations of tragedy dissolve ritual closure, preclude restoration.

Julia Kristeva's incisive analysis of abjection provides release from the constraints of a critical perspective that discovers the source of political recuperation and ritual restoration in the play's final act. Kristeva establishes a correspondence between a social *symbolic system* as it defines Law and the sacred and the specific structuration of the speaking subject within the *symbolic order*. Attempting to explain why a given *symbolic system* survives intact, Kristeva denies a cause and effect relation between Law and language, and thus avoids the problematic assumption of a pre-established divine order.[13] Chapter three argues that whereas the concept of the *pharmakos* condemns Racine's heroine to a final expunction, the more broadly defined *abjection* intensifies her presence within representation. The re-presentation of the *pharmakos* as the abject shows Law to be a disordering rather than an ordering principle.

The questionable status of women in Racine's theater is the subject of a separate chapter on the relation of narrative to history. More than background information for the ritual re-presentation of the history of their sacrifice, the women's narratives constitute their active presence. Examples from each of the mythic plays as well as from *Bérénice* and *Athalie* will demonstrate how the narrative situates the victim of ritual sacrifice within Law, excluded by the promise to imitate, as within art, present by virtue of her resistance to this promise. The power of the imagination cannot be separated in these texts from the history being described. Racine's female characters recount their suffering and indicate the source of their pain. The narrative is mimetic; its description objectifies the history of the heroine's sacrifice. Yet the art of narrating, the structures of repetition responsible for transforming history into a discourse performed on stage, elevates the status of women within Racine's patriarchal historiography. By describing her own loss or absence, the woman makes herself present to us; she establishes her portrait as the effect of her narrating. We, who must assume the role of the narratee, authenticate the woman's presence as as effect of her performance.[14]

Racine's heroine thus constitutes her otherness as integral to history. Reading *Britannicus* and *Bajazet* in the wake of a Derridean emphasis on *différence*, the final chapter develops a concept of Orientalism to elaborate further how the theater represents alterity within a world of likenesses. Neither realistic (descriptive) nor ornamental, the Oriental establishes the other within art as the model for the creating subject. With *Bajazet* tragedy completes its own cycle, for representation now authenticates the difference it formerly and formally sought to repress. This last chapter introduces Descartes as a character in his own right, the hero of this study's own representation of tragedy. While the *Discours* serves as a guide for reading the great book of the world, the philosopher himself enables us to confirm the truth of alterity thanks to his meticulous autobiographical account of his formulation of the analytical method. Descartes represents within critical discourse the same awareness of limits that motivates the hero's and heroine's efforts to know and determine themselves.

I have suggested above that one of the primary effects of this book's own representational cycle is to call special attention to a woman's difference. Feminist criticism has successfully elaborated a theory of gender distinctions based on the distribution of power within patriarchal society. From the Earth Mother to the matriarch, the woman consistently represents a potential for otherness which, for the men who conceptualize her as for the women who see themselves in their image, is linked to the idea of death.[15] The purpose of the readings which follow is not to reestablish the power of the patriarchy or to state again the case of women's subjugation. That such sexual politics is operant in Corneille's and Racine's writings hardly bears repeating. If the self-righteous anger that gave rise to this sort of criticism has taken us beyond repression and the pain that it engenders, the creative effort that allows us to find a source for pleasure in this tragedy is ongoing.[16] While there are doubtless those who will persist in saying that any subject constituted within the patriarchy is, by definition, compromised, I submit that the theater, by enabling us to distinguish between a woman's denied power and a woman's denial of patriarchal privilege, shows representation to affirm the possibility of a difference that is life. Throughout my readings of the plays of Corneille and Racine I argue not that a new brand of hero(ine)ism unseats the patriarch but rather that the woman's performance precludes metaphorical closure and the ordering of history into a paradigm of male power. Invalidating the standards of adequation which cause us to reason/rationalize the drama into a History of the Same, the woman decenters our perspective into the very uniform world of men who would see all in their own image.

Chapter One

Corneille's Tragedy in Perspective:
Le Cid, Horace, Cinna, Polyeucte

TRAGEDY IMPLIES AS ITS COROLLARY a sense of fulfillment that it cannot itself represent. The enactment of tragedy involves the separation of the individual from his coveted possession, the transformation of an inclusive desire into an exclusive choice. If tragedy lends itself particularly well to the theater, it is because of the unique perspective afforded by the stage. The audience's view of the performing characters serves to concretize the abstract relation of part to whole, loss to fulfillment. Viewed against the artful backdrop of successive scenes and acts as these give structure to life's experience, the characters' physical presence on the stage conveys the larger dimensions of the whole of the drama, the theater, and hence the world. The characters' suffering is created through the progressive and proportionate concentration of experience. Word and gesture gain significance as they are shown to reverberate within layers structuring the characters' conflict.

French classical tragedy, with its concern for Aristotelian unities and symmetrical design, is a prime example of this tightened structure. As the following study of Corneille's *Le Cid, Horace, Cinna,* and *Polyeucte* reveals, the action produces tension through direct confrontation, thereby exposing a unique reliance on boundary situations.[1] Through the duel of *Le Cid,* the debate of *Horace,* the trial of *Cinna,* and the martyrdom of *Polyeucte,* Corneille extends the hero's dialogue within the limits of the dialectical form.

If the classical model attempted to correct the excesses of the Renaissance, it conversely profited greatly from the Renaissance sense of order. The Renaissance perceived all experience, including the infinite, in terms of a circle, a closed geometric structure itself but one form of the divine order of creation.[2] This notion of absolute closure, in its implication of completeness reflected in the theater, may be used to explain how a tightening of rhetorical conventions in Corneille's plays can be shown to parallel his thematic movement towards the infinite.

In his *Corneille et la dialectique du héros* Serge Doubrovsky uses the Hegelian model to discuss the hero's progressive conquest of others in *Le Cid,* self in *Horace,* power in *Cinna,* and God in *Polyeucte.*[3] Underlying this kind of conflict, as it is exposed through the dialectical method, is what might be called a structural bipolarity that follows a corresponding development. *Bipolarity* means, in this context, the juxtaposition of two mutually repellent forms. The notion comprises the physical space of Corneille's theater, which tends to break down into halves. In the social perspective of the stage, the struggles of the aristocracy against the bourgeoisie suggest historic contradictions. These, Doubrovsky argues, are actually "transhistoric" because they expose an inalterable metaphysics, an "unchangeable" human dilemma.[4] Correspondingly, a study of the permutations of the bipolar model in Corneille's tragedies will be shown to extend the purely formal understanding of containment to an awareness of both infinity and finitude on the one hand and immortality and mortality on the other.

The successive stages in the hero's efforts to gain mastery over the father, the fatherland, the absolute power of the patriarchy, and God represent an incomplete movement along a unique hierarchy or chain of command. The hero's mastery is checked by his repeated encounters with an other force whose dominion increases from tragedy to tragedy. Thus if the hero's growth reflects a symmetrical formal design, the ultimate effect produced by this cycle of plays is strangely one of *décalage,* or sustained displacement. Indeed, the hero appears to be disproportionately figured, lacking a fixed identity, in Corneille's vertical extension of the metaphysical universe. The playwright denies a central locus of power by systematically expanding the theatrical space.

The bipolar structure responsible for containing the hero's energy shows the completion of an action to require an association of contraries. Each pole of the text must be interpreted in light of its opposite, and each individual text must be measured against the one which follows in sequence for the full meaning of Corneille's tragedy to be manifest. The latter association is not, strictly speaking, antonymic since the theme of each play remains the same quest for identity and authority within a politically limiting system. Still, the fact that the later play reopens the same questioning, albeit from a new plateau, suggests that the forms which bind the action in the first instance are reworked, again polarized, in the second. Perceived in the context of a cycle of representations, therefore, Corneille's persistent recourse to a bipolar structuring implies not the certitude of completion or the plenitude of forms but tension sustained through repetition.

This chapter will examine in detail the particular bipolar form that recurs in each play and it will trace how this binding form is restructured from one play to the other. Antonymic relations in *Le Cid* will be shown to be restructured in terms of paradigm in *Horace,* cycle in *Cinna,* and concentric orders in *Polyeucte.* Appreciable in terms of the operations of division, integration, substitution, and superimposition, respectively, the four tragedies depict the extension of the oppositional force into the vertical line, the full circle, and the circle within the circle. Corneille's representation of the universe is thus systematically reworked and refined. The form that becomes a line that becomes a circle and a circle within a circle is not, of course, visually perceptible on the stage any more than in the text. Yet the spectator of the performed tragedy, like its reader, must have a sense of dimension, of mass bearing down upon the hero, in order to comprehend the infinity in which the hero is enclosed.

To Open the Circle

The competing exigencies of love and honor impose a tragic choice on Rodrigue and Chimène. Responding to the influence of their respective fathers, the lovers enter into an adversarial relationship. The paternal mediation of their love is all the more confining because it is based on a shared system of values. Both Rodrigue and Chimène want to privilege the father's role; each agrees that the other must defend the father in order to be desired as a lover. It is the presence of two fathers, the mirroring of relations, that traps the lovers in a double bind. Models for each other's behavior, their reciprocal imitation allows for no escape. The dialectical form permits resolution only in sacrifice:

Réduit au triste choix ou de trahir ma flamme
Ou de vivre en infâme.[5]

The triangle of the couple's desires is viewed from all equally impossible sides through the fixed oppositions of the couplet form. Corneille's speeches delineate exclusive courses of action through what Albert Cook aptly describes as the confinement of "the plenum of emotion to the manifest recitation of its possible logical contrasts."[6] In Chimène's accusation of Rodrigue, for example, the couplet's rhyme suggests the full extent of the characters' differences:

> Ton honneur t'est plus cher que je ne te suis chère,
> Puisqu'il trempe tes mains dans le sang de mon père.
>   (V, i, 1509-10)

The separation of emotion into that felt by the *chère,* or beloved, and that exhibited towards the *père,* or honored loved one, captures the difficulty of Chimène's struggle. While she indicates her own vulnerability by sexualizing her role as *chère,* she represents her father as an immutable presence whose sexuality is subsumed by his political role. His absolute authority makes superfluous all adjectival qualification. The father is dead, and his death must be understood to be that of desire itself. Even the semantic similarities of the couplet's first line focus attention on a radical division. The parallelism of the signifiers *cher* and *chère,* suggesting the desire for unification, is denied by their signifieds: honor (*cher*) actually precludes love (*chère*). The difference in gender points to sexual opposition, failed union, despite shared passion.[7]

A like exclusivity is apparent in Rodrigue's evaluation of his plight:

> Je dois à ma maîtresse aussi bien qu'à mon père,
> J'attire en me vengeant sa haine et sa colère,
> J'attire ses mépris en ne me vengeant pas.
> A mon plus doux espoir l'un me rend infidèle
> Et l'autre indigne d'elle.
>   (I, vi, 322-26)

The first line of this passage posits the two sides of the conflict, which the following two lines discuss in turn. Incorporating the consequences of both courses of action, the concluding lines, however, subvert any attempt at synthesis. The sense of impasse is further reinforced by the extension of Don Diègue's earlier ultimatum—"Meurs ou tue" (I, v, 275)—into a complex series of negative options. If Rodrigue does not avenge his father, he loses his honor; if he loses his honor, he loses Chimène's respect.   The juxtapositions are multiple but the choices are consistently exclusive.[8]

The tension of the entire third act similarly derives from language whose symmetries paradoxically rend the text:

> Même soin me regarde et j'ai, pour m'affliger,
> Ma gloire à soutenir, et mon père à venger.
>
> (III, iv, 915-16)

We know that this is Chimène's explanation, but Corneille would have changed little had he given these lines to Rodrigue. The same values, the same dilemma, the same speeches fix the characters' separation.

In his recent rereading of this text, Doubrovsky argues that Rodrigue in fact destabilizes the dilemma. Proposing to Chimène that she avenge herself with his sword, Rodrigue would exchange the reciprocity of the duel for the dishonoring act of murder:

> "*Meurs ou tue*," certes, commandement quasi religieux, mais qui implique combat loyal, risque mutuel de vie, d'individu à individu (Rodrigue/le Comte) ou de groupe à groupe (Espagnols/Mores); bref: *affrontement d'homme à homme*. Mais non d'*homme à femme:* la relation cesse instantanément d'être réciproque.[9]

Even this rereading reverses but does not resolve the terms of the debate. Doubrovsky argues that Chimène cannot bring the affair to a satisfactory end without the intervention of a man. Yet this in no way changes the fact that Chimène, despite her limited power, dominates Rodrigue in this scene:

> Va, je suis ta partie, et non pas ton bourreau.
> Si tu m'offres ta tête, est-ce à moi de la prendre?
> Je la dois attaquer, mais tu dois la défendre.
>
> (940-42)

Rodrigue's "feminization" must be measured against Chimène's mastery/ "masculinization." If she refuses Rodrigue's sword, it is because *toute femme qu'elle est* she assumes no lack.

Chimène internalizes her struggle, experiencing it as a literal debate between her passion and her anger. To relieve the chaos of her mind, in which even logic takes the form of an emotion, she forces herself to dialogue with the signs of the rational world. This reading and interpreting of signs is the dialectical process through which are reasserted the oppositions of mind and body, inner and outer worlds, thoughts and emotions, passion and honor. Chimène proves the logic of fallacy, or loss, for she attempts to combat emotions through the very (logical) exchange that has set her at odds with herself:

> Silence, mon amour, laisse agir ma colère:
> S'il a vaincu deux rois, il a tué mon père;
> Ces tristes vêtements, où je lis mon malheur,
> Sont les premiers effets qu'ait produits sa valeur
> Et quoi qu'on die ailleurs d'un cœur si magnanime,
> Ici tous les objets me parlent de son crime.
> Vous qui rendez la force à mes ressentiments,
> Voiles, crêpes, habits, lugubres ornements,
> Pompe que me prescrit sa première victoire,
> Contre ma passion soutenez bien ma gloire
> Et lorsque mon amour prendra trop de pouvoir,
> Parlez à mon esprit de mon triste devoir,
> Attaquez sans rien craindre une main triomphante.
>   (IV, i, 1129-41)

If these mourning objects come to reify her emotions, it is because, as modern psychoanalysis confirms,[10] the loss of the love-object involves not only the disappearance of this object but also the subject's own loss of self:

> La moitié de ma vie a mis l'autre au tombeau,
> Et m'oblige à venger, après ce coup funeste,
> Celle que je n'ai plus sur celle qui me reste.
>   (III, iii, 800-02)

The balanced oppositions of this speech deny both the extension through likeness and the expansion through substitution which the later works exploit. Chimène sees her life uniquely as a function of the two dominant influences upon it. Prey to the contradictory demands of lover and father, she must endure the sacrifice that is her choice.

While *Horace* resembles *Le Cid* in its opposition of passion and honor, the Roman tragedy emphasizes less the incompatibility of orders than their similarity. Sabine depicts the battle between Rome and Albe as a confrontation of new and old histories in a unique tradition:

(Rome) Ingrate, souviens-toi que du sang de ses rois
Tu tiens ton nom, tes murs, et tes premières lois.
Albe est ton origine: arrête et considère
Que tu portes le fer dans le sein de ta mère.
(I, i, 53-56)

Qualifying war as matricide, the destruction of one's roots and nurture, the metaphor of these lines shows the hero to be oriented away from a conquest of other towards the conquest of the self. As Doubrovsky has observed, conquest in this tragic context is a paradox, for it means both fulfillment and suicide.[11] To engage in battle is to bring together, or integrate, one's potential selves as these are represented by the enemy. But the drama disintegrates the whole of the hero's mirrored selves, the ideal of his unique and indomitable power, in its double identification of victory with fratricide and fratricide with suicide. As Camille will insist through her own revolt against Horace, the glorious exercise of war can be readily deconstructed into the act through which the hero disembodies himself.

Linked in *amitié* through respect for Horace, *alliance* through the latter's marriage to his sister Sabine, and *amour* through his love for Camille, Horace's sister, Curiace insists on a proportionate and symmetrical relationship between family members who are thrice united:

...l'amitié, l'alliance et l'amour
Ne pourront empêcher que les trois Curiaces
Ne servent leur pays contre les trois Horaces.
(II, ii, 418-20)

Yet it is precisely this paradigm, Horace argues, which assures the hero victory. A man can accept to fight another because personal sacrifice assures him a bond with his father and the State. But beyond this real shedding of blood, glory is dependent on the hero's ability to abstract all the conditions which confront him into a single ideal:

Mais vouloir au public immoler ce qu'on aime,
S'attacher au combat *contre un autre soi-même,*
Attaquer un parti qui prend pour défenseur
Le frère d'une femme et l'amant d'une sœur
Et rompant tous ces nœuds, s'armer pour la patrie
Contre un sang qu'on voudrait racheter de sa vie,

        Une telle vertu n'appartenait qu'à nous.
        (II, iii, 443-49; emphasis mine)

Horace views the exceptional, or heroic, quality of his mission precisely in the opportunity it provides to negate the other, to meet patriotic demands so as to deny the distinction of self-family-country-virtue. War is an act of self-possession. It is the means through which the individual elevates himself to the superhuman, or divine. Establishing a paradigm of indivisible selves, this passage reveals what Doubrovsky terms "the tragic necessity of affirming superiority in identity."[12]

In Horace's speech a metaphor of blindness suggests the repression of all difference. Describing his response to the king's command that he fight the Albains, Horace insists that he willfully acts to suppress any identity but his own. By imposing anonymity on the enemy he previously knew as Curiace, Horace discovers an extension of himself in his opponent:

        Contre qui que ce soit que mon pays m'emploie,
        J'accepte aveuglément cette gloire avec joie <...>
        Albe vous a nommé, je ne vous connais plus.
        (491-502)

Curiace finds this behavior abhorrent: "Je vous connais encore, et c'est ce qui me tue" (503). Ultimately, however, Curiace accepts to be drawn into the battle whose undistinguishable lines his own speech has fashioned:

        De tous les deux côtés j'ai des pleurs à répandre;
        De tous les deux côtés mes désirs sont trahis.
        (II, i, 396-97)

Both men assert a unique and identical identity for themselves and their countries. This oneness, however, is not real but rather the effect of their representation. The metaphor of sameness correlates with a male perception, a perspective whose arbitrariness is exposed by the play's female characters. Identity requires that one be recognized by another.[13] This situation, too, proves tragic for the hero who, in his bid to assimilate the other, eliminates the very source of his own prestige. Curiace strikes a chord when he accuses Horace of becoming an instrument of the State: "Je rends grâces aux Dieux de n'être pas Romain, / Pour conserver encor quelque chose d'humain" (II, iii, 481-82). But it is the women in this play who most effectively thwart the heroic enterprise, for they refuse to reflect back to the hero the image that he would establish for himself.

Sabine remains outside the Roman identity that she has assumed in marriage. She looks beyond the man to the situation that engages him, beyond the single victory to the loss that it defines:

> Je m'attache un peu moins aux intérêts d'un homme:
> Je ne suis point pour Albe et ne suis plus pour Rome,
> Je crains pour l'une et l'autre en ce dernier effort
> Et serai du parti qu'affligera le sort.
> Egale à tous les deux jusques à la victoire,
> Je prendrai part aux maux sans en prendre à la gloire
> Et je garde, au milieu de tant d'âpres rigueurs,
> Mes larmes aux vaincus et ma haine aux vainqueurs.
>
> (I, i, 87-94)

Camille further denies both a man's identity and his place. The Father's Law is reappropriated by her act of recognition. The feminine perspective refuses the hero's status, for it conflates the standards used to judge him:

> Mais si près d'un hymen, l'amant que donne un père
> Nous est moins qu'un époux et non pas moins qu'un frère.
>
> (III, iv, 887-88)

A woman's perspective is double; her power is an ability to discern differences. If the men work from an essential likeness to a global vision, the women know wholeness to depend on the harmony of discrete elements. It is to the integrity of individuals and of individual causes that the woman devotes herself.

The women share this perspective, yet, as if to dramatize further its dual nature, they disagree with each other. Camille claims that she has lost her point of reference, that she has fallen, as it were, from representation:

> Ainsi, ma sœur, du moins vous avez dans vos plaintes
> Où porter vos souhaits et terminer vos craintes.
>
> (891-92)

Sabine, however, assures Camille that the very lack of determinacy which she experiences is a potential for action. Though she preaches obedience,

Sabine actually gives impetus to Camille's revolt by freeing her from the constraints of the male configuration of power. That is, Sabine's defense of Horace inadvertently engages her in a refutation of his paradigm of indivisible selves:

> Mais l'amant qui vous charme et pour qui vous brûlez
> Ne vous est, après tout, que ce que vous voulez.
>
> (905-06)

Sabine does not intend her remarks to influence negatively the hero's stature. Nor does she herself wish to appropriate the hero's role. Yet she has made a statement that prevents us from interpreting her admonishment to Camille as a sign of feminine passivity: "Si l'on fait moins qu'un homme, on fait plus qu'une femme" (I, i, 12). Sabine advocates that Camille support her blood relation at the expense of her lover. Still, in what might be an attempt to secure a vicarious pleasure, she gives Camille the option of determining herself.

Camille becomes more than a passive woman. If, as Mitchell Greenberg argues, Sabine creates a space for herself that cannot be fully accommodated by society, a "space that is neither a man's nor a woman's but is somewhere 'in between,' "[14] Camille moves to inhabit this space and to make it a woman's. Interestingly, the logic of Camille's revolt is elaborated by her sister-in-law's counsel against it. Camille takes Sabine at her word but pushes the meaning of this word further still:

> Ce que peut le caprice, osez-le par raison,
> Et laissez votre sang hors de comparaison.
>
> (III, iv, 909-10)

Camille does endeavor to make Horace "beyond comparison"; that is, she places him outside of metaphor. She does so, moreover, by "leaving her blood" so that it stains the model, denies the chain of resemblances—the comparisons—which constitute it. Camille's revolt involves a rational choice whose coherence successfully undermines the integrity of the heroic model. The perfect act—unparalleled, unequaled, *beyond compare*— is a consummation. It precludes completion in a second movement.[15] Deliberately provoking Horace to kill her, Camille forces a comparison. By virtue of its double nature, however, this second act cannot be assimilated into the male paradigm:

> Voir le dernier Romain à son dernier soupir,
> Moi seule en être cause, et mourir de plaisir!
> (IV, v, 1317-18)

The controlling I/eye here is Camille's; her perspective regulates this crucial scene. Distinguishing herself from Horace's eternal Rome, Camille denies the absolute quality of *patrie* as a final determinant:

> Rome, l'unique objet de mon ressentiment!
> Rome, à qui vient ton bras d'immoler mon amant!
> Rome qui t'a vu naître, et que ton cœur adore!
> Rome enfin que je hais parce qu'elle t'honore!
> (1301-04)

Camille doubly degrades Horace. Negating the singularity of the standard of perfection with which he identifies (Rome as universal), she refuses the sufficiency of his one act. Camille, moreover, undermines Horace's claim to exceptional behavior by utilizing her place outside the paradigm which he invokes to measure his glory. Punctuating the anaphora of these lines, her death is the break in the text that topples the male hierarchy and sends it back to its maternal roots, back to Albe and its mother's breast.

Compensating for *Horace*'s vertical movement of dis/integration, *Cinna* re-presents the hero's evolution in terms of a cycle. Yet the hero in this play achieves no further mastery; he remains alienated within the history that takes shape around him. Measuring his identity against a world of shifting appearances, the hero's rise to the top of the chain of command is complicated by Corneille's reformulation of the hierarchical power structure into a history whose rotating motion perpetually leaves the hero one step behind knowledge and individual identity. *Horace* has depicted heroism in terms of the self's unification with the other. Now *Cinna* precludes the very possibility of unification by its insistence on the multiplicity of this other.

Seeking vengeance for those whose deaths assured Auguste's rise to power, the conspirators continue the same mercenary tactics that had earlier plunged Rome into a state of civil war. They corrupt the new order by secretly plotting against Auguste. Obscuring his efforts to absolve the past, they entangle the empire in a web of uncertainty and deceit. Although intended as corrective or compensatory gestures, the conspirators' actions are themselves inadequate. Their duplicity perpetuates a history still incomplete and unresolved.

Emilie roots the struggle for vengeance in a crude materialism:

> Quoique j'aime Cinna, quoique mon cœur l'adore,
> S'il me veut *posséder,* Auguste doit périr,
> Sa tête est le seul *prix* dont il peut m'acquérir <...>
> Et des mêmes *présents* qu'il (Auguste) *verse* dans mes mains
> J'*achète* contre lui les esprits des Romains <...>
> Pour qui venge son père il n'est point de forfaits,
> Et c'est *vendre* son sang que se rendre aux bienfaits.
>
>   (I, ii, 54-84; emphasis mine)

Like Chimène, Emilie risks her love in order to protect her father's honor. But Emilie enjoys an option unavailable to Chimène at the time of her crisis. Emilie can reasonably postulate that vengeance will not require her to sacrifice. This fact does not challenge her sincerity; rather it accentuates the cool pragmatism governing her emotions. In the mercenary world that Emilie represents, an object is appreciated not in and of itself but for its exchange value, i.e. the *other* for which it can be substituted. The power of her speech rests precisely on its doubling of conditions as so many signifiers. She denies metaphorical closure through a continual alternation which allows her to slip—metonymically—from one relation to another.

In terms of rhetorical conventions the principle of exchange extends from metaphor as it implies the continuity between one object and another. The subversion of paradigmatic forms into contiguous relations (the extension of the metaphoric pattern to the metonymic) creates a cycle of signifiers that diversify rather than synthesize experience. Such diversification is designed to counterbalance the emperor's absolute power. By insisting on a principle of indigenous leadership in evidence across the world, Maxime attempts to persuade Auguste to abdicate:

> J'ose dire, Seigneur, que par tous les climats
> Ne sont pas bien reçus toutes sortes d'Etats,
> Chaque peuple a le sien conforme à sa nature,
> Qu'on ne saurait changer sans lui faire une injure:
> Telle est la loi du ciel, dont la sage équité
> Sème dans l'univers cette diversité.
>
>   (II, i, 535-40)

And Cinna, pretending to defend Auguste, explains the unprecedented growth of absolutism in terms of an inevitable course of events:

> Il est vrai que du ciel la prudence infinie
> Départ à chaque peuple un différent génie,
> Mais il n'est pas moins vrai que cet ordre des cieux
> Change selon les temps comme selon les lieux.
>   (545-48)[16]

The conspirators' tactics effectively frustrate Auguste. The persistent flux of circumstances continually requires him to redefine his world. Unable to stabilize his perceptions, Auguste fails to secure an absolute power:

> J'ai souhaité l'empire, et j'y suis parvenu,
> Mais en le souhaitant, je ne l'ai pas connu,
> Dans sa possession j'ai trouvé pour tous charmes
> D'effroyables soucis, d'éternelles alarmes,
> Mille ennemis secrets, la mort à tous propos,
> Point de plaisir sans trouble, et jamais de repos.
>   (371-76)

In an agonizing moment Auguste comes to accept death as his only means for influencing the course of events. His authority is limited to participation in the deceptions that rule his life. Death is his revenge, a last exchange in the series of substitutions that have thwarted his command:

> Meurs et dérobe-lui la gloire de ta chute,
> Meurs, tu ferais pour vivre un lâche et vain effort <...>
> Meurs, puisque c'est un mal que tu ne peux guérir,
> Meurs enfin, puisqu'il faut ou tout perdre, ou mourir <...>
> Meurs, mais quitte du moins la vie avec éclat.
>   (IV, ii, 1170-79)

Although each line depicts a different rationale, the consequence of the various logical forms is the persistent call to death. These lines thus form a series of interchangeable arguments which gain no greater significance. They become no more absolute for being considered together. Finding resolution only in death, Auguste expresses the need to abandon the self for the other in a final break with the hope of experiencing the infinite in the real.

Polyeucte similarly gives himself over to the other, but with the hope of realizing an absolute power though a real sacrifice. This inversion suggests the two poles of the latter play's tragedy, for the question of Polyeucte's success remains unresolved by critical debate. André Stegmann discovers in *Polyeucte* the "fusion intime (d'une intrigue amoureuse et d'un sacrifice sacré), l'amour jeune, noble, profond du couple Pauline-Polyeucte donnant l'enracinement charnel à la conversion éclatante du héros et à ses conséquences."[17] Consistent with Nadal and Doubrovsky, who instead maintain that Corneille challenges the finality of the tragedy's Christian resolution, I submit that the play's oppositions force a distinction between the heroic and the saintly.[18] Polyeucte's baptism, the martyrdom of Polyeucte and Néarque, and the conversions of Pauline and Félix mark the Christian intent of the playwright who wrote in his *Dédicace à la Reine Régente* (1643) that *Polyeucte* would speak to her of God. The play's Christian elements cannot, however, adequately account for Polyeucte's heroic ambitions. Corneille superimposes the saintly ideal on the heroic model but provides no final synthesis of the sacred and the profane.

The argument for a Christian tragedy is not to be dismissed. Instead, the play's overtly Christian theme must be reevaluated in light of its consequences for the heroic enterprise. Though it closes the play on a note of Christian faith that is a promise to proselytize, Félix's speech nonetheless stands as testimony of the gap remaining between new and old religions:

> Allons à nos martyrs donner la sépulture,
> Baiser leurs corps sacrés, les mettre en digne lieu,
> Et faire retentir partout le nom de Dieu.
>   (V, vi, 1812-14)

The sacred act of devotion does not yet correspond to the name of God. The "Et" of this particular speech, one of many in evidence throughout the play, suggests not only the insufficiency of what has come before but also how removed the all-important issue of a saintly choice is from a hero's act of sacrifice. The prominence of the connective *and* in *Polyeucte* contrasts markedly with the either/or propositions of *Le Cid:*

> Je méprise sa crainte, *et* je cède à ses larmes.
>   (I, i, 17; emphasis mine)

Je sens déjà mon cœur prêt à se révolter,
Et ce n'est qu'en fuyant que j'y puis résister.
(I, ii, 123-24; emphasis mine)

And in these instances implies a movement contrary to appearances. Polyeucte gives the impression of sympathy while at the same time distancing himself from the scene. The conjunction helps to structure a layer of devotion with which to cover his egoism. The play intends Polyeucte's election of divine over earthly love as a serious commitment. It is a commitment, however, that does not require a choice. Polyeucte can find both love *and* glory in a martyr's death that is far more accessible than a hero's sacrifice.

The events surrounding his baptism, like those of his death, evidence an ego intent on its own satisfaction. Indeed, the very concept of conversion is problematic, for Polyeucte appears to continue along a unique path to personal glory. From this point of view, martyrdom is an act of self-indulgence:

Néarque
Mais dans ce temple enfin la mort est assurée.
Polyeucte
Mais dans le ciel déjà la palme est préparée.
(II, vi, 661-62)[19]

Polyeucte's objection to Néarque provides an interesting contrast with one he makes to Pauline earlier:

Je vous aime,
Le ciel m'en soit témoin, cent fois plus que moi-même,
Mais...
(I, ii, 113-15)

The ellipsis makes secret his devotion to God: "But I love my God more than I love even you, Pauline." To this he now adds "For to love my God is to realize a personal glory that means more to me than life itself." Polyeucte's silence in the first instance is telling.

It is not Christianity that Corneille challenges here but rather the notion of love and one's ability to give of oneself in defense of an ideal. And Polyeucte demonstrates a propensity for exchange reminiscent of

Emilie. He seeks to impose on Pauline a compromise love in order to assure his total satisfaction:

> Mon amour par pitié cherche à vous soulager:
> Il voit quelle douleur dans l'âme vous possède,
> Et sait qu'un autre amour en est le seul remède.
> (V, iii, 1586-88)

The mutual constancy of Pauline and Sévère's love is one of the outstanding fusions which the play offers. Realized, however, as a substitute for Pauline's love for Polyeucte, it works against a sense of harmony. The conjunction "Et," reinforced here by the adjective "autre," points to the inadequacy of both Polyeucte's proposal of love to Pauline (a protestation of fidelity which promises infidelity) and his love of God, for neither suffices alone. Although Polyeucte is convinced of the superiority of his gesture, his failure to avoid sacrificing Pauline to his own glory undermines the saintliness of his mission to God. His pity is patronizing. And his plea to Pauline that she preserve his memory on earth, sign of human vanity, confounds only further the issue of a divine calling:

> A la gloire.
> Chère Pauline, adieu, conservez ma mémoire.
> (1679-80)

Polyeucte is as concerned with his personal fortune as with serving his Maker. Reaching for God, he discovers his soul in a saintly martyrdom. But he seeks a hero's triumph through a death that contradicts it. No longer focusing on challenges to be met in this world, Polyeucte allows himself a facile escape to heaven. The saint's ascension is the sign of the hero's fall:

> Pourquoi mettre au hasard ce que la mort assure?
> Quand elle ouvre le ciel, peut-elle sembler dure?
> (II, vi, 665-66)[20]

Corneille's representation of the hero's fate is a significant departure from the pure representation of harmony in the Renaissance. Based on what Poulet terms "retour," the Renaissance model assumed perfection in completeness:

> Le corps en retournant à la matière, l'âme en retournant à Dieu, accomplissent donc l'un et l'autre un cercle et un cycle. Mais le retour de l'âme à Dieu n'est pas seulement représentable sous la forme d'un mouvement périphérique. Dieu, cercle infini que l'âme envahit et parcourt, est aussi Dieu, centre infini où elle s'enfonce. Le retour de l'âme est un retour au centre. Point de départ, le centre est aussi point d'aboutissement.[21]

Such is the experience of the saintly Polyeucte. Corneille, however, doubles the circle: he locks the saint in a hero's body. Enclosing the supposedly infinite circle within the hero's world, the playwright shows the Renaissance construct to be a product of man's imagination, an expression of faith contradicted by experience. Meaning is not a culmination as it extends from a Renaissance-styled analogic chain[22] but the issuing forth of new knowledge of limits and the recognition of man's insufficiency. The death that paves the way to heaven in *Polyeucte* pierces a hole at the center of the hero's universe. Here, as is the case for each of the plays in this series, the final act is destined to sustain the very tensions that it pretends to resolve. Closure is, in a word, open.

Unresolving

Writing on the concept of closure in his editor's preface to the *Yale French Studies* issue devoted to the subject, David F. Hult comments:

> "Closure" comes to interrogate not simply predetermined units (those "having" an end) but rather what it is that manages to determine or delimit a given artistic unit, what in fact defines and constitutes its very boundaries. Thus, to make a simple but useful equation: "End" is to "meaning" as "closure" is to "interpretation."[23]

The preceding investigation into the enclosed world of Corneille's theater likewise presumes an interest in more than a movement towards completion. The insistence on closure does not restrict the diversity of all that exists within this space. On the contrary, as a result of the expansion of the plays' formal boundaries, the signifying chain grows larger within the circumscribed limits of the text. Signifiers are continually multiplied within

a closed system of referents. The discovery of each limit and of each truth
assures our distance from the Truth. Corneille's plays consequently lead by
their own logic to a discussion of closure as interpretation.

To avoid the impression of compromise, Don Fernand justifies his
decision to reunite Chimène and Rodrigue on the grounds that history is not
an independent moment but a succession of moments, each of whose
meaning is multiplied by association with the others. The final test of an act
is not its competency, its success in meeting certain criteria, but its
resistance or resiliency before the transforming effects of time:

> Le temps assez souvent a rendu légitime
> Ce qui semblait d'abord ne se pouvoir sans crime.
> (V, vii, 1813-14)

In the space of a year Chimène will have paid her respects to her
father. And Rodrigue will be all the more deserving of her hand after
another year's service in defense of the country. Nevertheless, the king's
final judgment fails to resolve the ambiguities of this scene. Rodrigue, who
repeats many of his earlier protestations, appeals to Chimène that she
avenge herself. He solicits a response for which he knows her incapable
because the response, like the appeal, sustains the tortured necessity of an
unacceptable choice:

> Prenez une vengeance à tout autre impossible.
> Mais du moins que ma mort suffise à me punir:
> Ne me bannisez point de votre souvenir
> Et puisque mon trépas conserve votre gloire,
> Pour vous en revancher conservez ma mémoire
> Et dites quelquefois, en déplorant mon sort:
> "S'il ne m'avait aimée, il ne serait pas mort."
> (1794-1800)

For her part, Chimène acknowledges the hero's presence but fails to
address him directly: "Relève-toi Rodrigue. Il faut l'avouer, Sire" (1801).
Referring to Rodrigue but representing him only to the king, Chimène's
speech brings us away from a fixed history, away from the model of
heroism forged by Don Fernand:

Rodrigue a des vertus que je ne puis haïr
Et quand un roi commande, on lui doit obéir.
Mais à quoi que déjà vous m'ayez condamnée,
Pourrez-vous à vos yeux souffrir cet hyménée?
Et quand de mon devoir vous voulez cet effort,
Toute votre justice en est-elle d'accord?
Si Rodrigue à l'Etat devient si nécessaire,
De ce qu'il fait pour vous dois-je être le salaire
Et me livrer moi-même au reproche éternel
D'avoir trempé mes mains dans le sang paternel?
(1803-12)

Thus although in the king's discourse history provides for an exchange of roles and allows the couple to reverse the effects of the past, the making of this history—its representation on stage—is revealed to be a dialectical process, ongoing and discontinuous.

Horace problematizes the question of history still further. By subjecting a single act to divergent explanations, the characters of this tragedy place the question of heroism squarely within the bounds of interpretation and beyond descriptive representation. Indeed, Horace's need to refute this notion provides a poignant testimony of its power. The hero's glory depends on his ability to isolate standards of purity and perfection within a tainted history that mirrors success in failure:

Le peuple, qui voit tout seulement par l'écorce,
S'attache à son effet pour juger de sa force,
Il veut que ses dehors gardent un même cours,
Qu'ayant fait un miracle, elle en fasse toujours.
Après une action pleine, haute, éclatante,
Tout ce qui brille moins remplit mal son attente,
Il veut qu'on soit égal en tout temps, en tous lieux,
Il n'examine point si lors on pouvait mieux,
Ni que, s'il ne voit pas sans cesse une merveille,
L'occasion est moindre, et la vertu pareille.
(V, ii, 1559-68)

Justifying the principle of exchange that Horace rejects, Tulle is able to save the hero from himself:

Ce crime, quoique grand, énorme, inexcusable,
Vient de la même épée et part du même bras
Qui me fait aujourd'hui maître de deux Etats.
                                        (V, iii, 1740-42)

The enactment of history provides no synthesis except in its shift of power from the hero to the monarch. Without excusing the crime, Tulle judges it to be less consequential than Horace's previous victory. Fratricide is suppressed in an act of paternalism that synthesizes the contradictory events of the past into a single history of the State. By Tulle's own admission, this kind of judgment is a dissembling, for its execution requires that the crime itself be ignored. We find here another example of the metaphorical power of the play. Greenberg signals the transformation of a man "into an ideal—duty, glory, honor—which, in turn, is recuperated as the reflexion of the dominant ideology of the State."[24] An ideological history comes to substitute for legend:

De pareils serviteurs sont les forces des rois,
Et de pareils aussi sont au-dessus des lois.
Qu'elles se taisent donc, que Rome dissimule
Ce que dès sa naissance elle vit en Romule.
                                        (1753-56)

Even this new ideology is an illusion, for no act is totalizing. Tulle's clemency extends to Camille, whom he orders be interred with Curiace. Though it assures the continuity of the same singular order, the double burial memorializes Camille's difference by affording her status:

Je la plains, et pour rendre à son sort rigoureux
Ce que peut souhaiter son esprit amoureux,
Puisqu'en un même jour l'ardeur d'un même zèle
Achève le destin de son amant et d'elle,
Je veux qu'un même jour, témoin de leurs deux morts,
En un même tombeau voie enfermer leurs corps.
                                        (1777-82)

Camille becomes an equal partner of history. Her tragedy, too, is perfected, for she completes here the dispersion of meaning, the deconstruction of metaphor, begun with her assault against Horace. Greenberg argues that the "tragedy of origins and difference, of symmetry and State, ends in the establishment of a new, triumphant order of the same. Camille is put where she did not want to be, in the same place/grave as Curiace. The two are made One."[25] But Camille has carved out this place for herself. Significantly, it is a place that prevents us from viewing the actions of the play as uniform. Camille goes to her grave much like a bride to the altar. A fusion of the marriage and the funeral ceremonies cannot be realized, however, because time violates all synthesis. Enjoying only a posthumous union with Curiace, Camille is and is not a wife. Her presence in the tomb represents a violation of the marriage bed. Still, one cannot say that this is where Camille does not want to be. For here, as in her earlier revolt against Horace, Camille experiences a rift in the identification process that submits her to the male model. Camille acquires status as part of Tulle's decision to honor Horace. Yet the hero's action towards her cannot be understood except in response to her own provocation. Camille's privilege is therefore not that of a man's woman. Her challenge to Horace has forged— forced—a final resting place where she never assumes (in marriage) the name of Curiace. Hers is properly an isolated space *beside* the Other, a space that bears her name alone.

Entering the paternal metaphor only after her life is spent, Camille is never really one with those who would make her the same (*même*). To be recognized after death by the system whose law threatens her identity—to be ceremoniously honored by society's leader—assures, moreover, Camille's sustained presence in history. The play's final scene is less a sacrifice of her difference than a tribute to it. Entombed with her lover, Camille represents the violation of all synthesis, the triumph of diversity and dissension within a tradition of arbitrary oneness.

In *Cinna* the break between objective and subjective readings of history is even more pronounced. To interpret is to forget as an act of conscience. Livie persuades Auguste that absolution is within the power of the leader who acts as a son of God:

> Tous ces crimes d'Etat qu'on fait pour la couronne,
> Le ciel nous en absout alors qu'il nous la donne,
> Et dans le sacré rang où sa faveur l'a mis,
> Le passé devient juste et l'avenir permis.
>   (V, ii, 1609-12)

Memory has failed to provide continuity. Although exposed to numerous examples of generosity, Cinna refuses to model himself after them:

> Tu t'en souviens, Cinna: tant d'heur et tant de gloire
> Ne peuvent pas sitôt sortir de ta mémoire.
> Mais ce qu'on ne pourrait jamais s'imaginer,
> Cinna, tu t'en souviens, et veux m'assassiner.
>   (V, i, 1473-76)

Auguste counteracts these effects through a "magnanimous forgetting" (*oubli magnanime*) (V, iii, 1733). Clemency is a refusal to remember, the assurance of a "Horatian" victory through a revolutionary decision to judge from the perspective of the future:

> Je suis maître de moi comme de l'univers,
> Je le suis; je veux l'être. O siècles, ô mémoire,
> Conservez à jamais ma dernière victoire!
>   (V, iii, 1696-98)

As his admonishment of Cinna makes clear, what finally gives Auguste the edge over the conspirators is his incorporation of interpretation into the dialectical process as another level of exchange:

> Ta fortune est bien haut, tu peux ce que tu veux,
> Mais tu ferais pitié même à ceux qu'elle irrite,
> Si je t'abandonnais à ton peu de mérite.
> Ose me démentir, dis-moi ce que tu vaux,
> Conte-moi tes vertus, tes glorieux travaux,
> Les rares qualités par où tu m'as dû plaire,
> Et tout ce qui t'élève au-dessus du vulgaire.
> Ma faveur fait ta gloire, et ton pouvoir en vient:
> Elle seule t'élève et seule te soutient.
>   (V, i, 1520-28)

Auguste understands the power of exchange to be that of choice. It is a ruler's privilege, the expression of the divine power of creation. For to decide Cinna's fate is to determine values and fix meanings for society. In order to condemn any abuse of authority, Corneille has Auguste play by the same rules as his subjects. But he endows the emperor with a superior skill.

In *Polyeucte* a deliberate withholding of judgment makes of history an interpretative process. Fact becomes, quite literally, an act of faith.

Tolerance, the moral equivalent of an unresolved dialectic, sustains the play's double layers of meaning:

> Qui ne serait touché d'un si tendre spectacle?
> De pareils changements ne vont point sans miracle <...>
> J'approuve cependant que chacun ait ses Dieux,
> Qu'il les serve à sa mode, et sans peur de la peine.
>
> (V, vi, 1787-99)

Even Félix's final appeal for Christian unification does not counter the monarch's explicit defense of Christianity as the other religion. As rightfully would befit a character with the name Sévère, his policy of tolerance reasserts a radical division of pagan and Christian, hero and saint.

If the text exposes through this call to interpretation its own signifying process, the theater is more than the representation of this process. The possibility of self-referentiality does not make the text transparent but, on the contrary, increases ambivalences and locates meaning in an interpretation that is itself subject to persistent restructurings. The hero's evolution from play to play is a rite of passage into a world whose dimensions are more vast than those of the one he leaves behind. As the following chapter will argue through a focus on taboo and ritual, this is a rite which, if it gradually frees the hero from constraints, systematically deprives him of the protection that these provide. The geometry of the doubled structures, designating the space of the horizontal plane, the vertical plane, the circle, and concentric circles, provides no point of coincidence. There is no completion, because the forms are consistently reconceived. There is no fatality since all things—including this formulation—are reversible. For Corneille the closed system is constantly redefined and tested. The enclosure of the theatrical space has been made coordinate with the theme it displays.

Chapter Two

The Mask Behind the Sacred

THE FULLNESS OF THE THEATRICAL EXPERIENCE, the sequential expansion of its ontological space, is not sustained by the tragedies which follow *Polyeucte*. The hero, the heroic code, and the belief in man's glorious destiny all begin to crumble. By *Rodogune* violence is endemic. Acts of sacrifice succeed only in further entangling relations between characters and in further confounding moral choices.

Although not posited in terms of ritual sacrifice, the previous chapter has shown *Le Cid, Horace, Cinna,* and *Polyeucte* each to create a hero through an act of sacrifice—the very need to choose implicit in the dialectical form. Rodrigue's valor issues from his conviction that love must be sacrificed for duty. Horace prepares to meet his death in battle and again before his king, confident that even Camille's murder cannot detract from his victory against Albe. From Horace's point of view, the testimony he presents to defend his name constitutes another personal sacrifice whose benefits are finally reaped in the king's accord. Cinna risks his life to please his lover and undertakes the violent action of the conspiracy to persuade his countrymen and eventually Auguste himself of the monarchy's indiscriminate government. Last in this series, Polyeucte, his death the necessary model for the conversion of pagan society to Christianity, enjoys the pleasure of his own transcendence.

We have noted, however, that the effects of sacrifice are dulled somewhat by the plays' resolutions. In the first three plays the prince's intervention precludes the necessity of a final choice for the hero, and this act of generosity is, paradoxically, responsible for making the role of sacrifice in Corneille's historiography all the more ambiguous. *Polyeucte,* meanwhile, further confounds the idea of sacrifice through the hero's purely private satisfaction of desire. In his speech we hear resonances of Horace's self-righteous defense of his honor. Indeed, if these early tragedies together represent a unique ritual, the repetition of ritual activity from one play to another merely accentuates the ongoing struggle of personal and public interests.

Chimène, Camille, and to a lesser degree, Emilie and Pauline have exposed the problematics of this ritual activity. Each (albeit for a different reason) thwarts the hero's bid for glory by claiming for herself the same right to sacrifice. But it takes another woman, *Rodogune*'s Cléopâtre, to refute the cause of heroism entirely. Turning first to *Rodogune,* and then to *Héraclius* and *Œdipe,* this chapter will explore in the specific context of ritual activity the consequences of the cyclical patterning produced through the dialectical form. Corneille's structuring of ritual will be studied in light of Girard's model for sacrifice as a unique act of violence that prevents the explosion of society into reciprocal acts of vengeance. Focusing particularly on the role of the double analyzed by Girard, the readings of the plays will emphasize the importance of repeated substitutions. However, these exchanges will be shown to bring the characters to acts of transgression. Contrary to Girard's belief in restorative violence, ritual in Corneille denies the capacity of (the Father's) Law to harmonize society.

Ritual in Crisis: *Rodogune*

Rodogune exposes the ritual process in excruciating detail, yet it offers no final harmony. The drama blocks the attainment of the sublime, corrupts the sense of mission. It denigrates the monarchy through Cléopâtre's self-serving directives. Heroes are replaced by nonheroes as the division between good and evil becomes, paradoxically, more clearly discernible and increasingly less easy to maintain. The play creates a double-bind situation through a series of propositions/ultimatums. In Act I Cléopâtre's promised divulgence of the twins' order of birth establishes birthright as the criterion for both succession to the throne and marriage to Rodogune. The possibility of one brother's double satisfaction is eliminated, however, in Act II by Cléopâtre's new stipulation that Rodogune's death be the price paid for the throne. And it is further threatened in Act III when Rodogune establishes Cléopâtre's death as her own condition for love. In this complicated scenario one brother necessarily loses all, while the other's potential gain is doubly qualified by his twin's sacrifice and the need to choose either between power and love (Act II) or between sensual and maternal love (Act III). Yet the resolving action corresponds to none of the solutions allowed for by the propositions. Neither Cléopâtre's murder of Séleucus nor her suicide is a response for which the ultimatums provided. Moreover, Antiochus's and Rodogune's consequent accession to power is contrary to Cléopâtre's every wish and constitutes a merely superficial satisfaction of Rodogune's plan for vengeance. Cléopâtre is dead, but by her own hand—neither brother has actively sought to undermine her. The process of signification thus extends beyond the crisis resolved through sacrifice. Corneille relocates tragedy in the sacred: a primal scream resounds inside the space delimited by ritual.

Two opposing patterns structure the drama. Shifting, or change, corresponds to a differentiation process that establishes a hierarchy (represented by the exclusive power of the throne), while stasis is depicted through balanced forms (represented by the twins). The hierarchic ordering, or ranking, of forms and the lateral juxtaposition, or doubling, of forms are inverse functions which radically divide the text. Each dynamic is exhaustive in and of itself: vertical shifting defines a historical progression that is tyranny; parallel relations depict a stagnation that is the end of the natural cycle. Although resolution of the political crisis depends on the elimination of a (sacrificial) victim, this violence merely accentuates the conflict following the crisis.

The play's opening promise of festive rejoicing is but a cover for Cléopâtre's real intentions. Laonice's expressed faith in an end to vengeance and a secure peace unwittingly relates the truth about Cléopâtre's arbitrary control of the twins' fate. Cléopâtre has kept open the question of legitimate succession in order to manipulate these circumstances to her own advantage:

> Ce grand jour est venu, mon frère, où notre reine,
> Cessant de plus tenir la couronne incertaine,
> Doit rompre aux yeux de tous son silence obstiné,
> De deux princes gémeaux nous déclarer l'aîné;
> Et l'avantage seul d'un moment de naissance,
> Dont elle a jusqu'ici caché la connaissance,
> Mettant au plus heureux le sceptre dans la main,
> Va faire l'un sujet, et l'autre souverain.
>
> (I, i, 7-14)

Nature produces identical twins. Cléopâtre, however, works against nature's balance to establish the absolute dominance of one brother over, and at the expense of, the other. Insensitive and unscrupulous, Cléopâtre gives herself over to a form of truly Machiavellian politics:

> Je fis beaucoup alors, et ferais encor plus
> S'il était quelque voie, infâme ou légitime,
> Que m'enseignât la gloire ou que m'ouvrît le crime,
> Qui me pût conserver un bien que j'ai chéri
> Jusqu'à verser pour lui tout le sang d'un mari.
>   (II, ii, 470-74)

The maternal presence is monstrous. But if to measure difference within the political spectrum uniquely in terms of superiority and inferiority is condemnable, so too is nature's failure to assert any difference at all. To preclude distinction is to preclude heroism as survival itself. The play develops the twins' identicalness as a sign of a pernicious inaction, a lack of initiative and self-determination that fosters Cléopâtre's criminal design. The twins will fail to exercise the autonomy that Cléopâtre would anyway deny them.

Pushed to the extreme, a deterioration of the natural cycling into a process of duplication is incest. Indeed, incest is an abstract limit—a transgression implied by, but not explicitly incorporated into, the text. In the original account by Appian of Alexandria, Cléopâtre kills her husband for having married Rodogune and, to avenge herself further, marries his brother Antiochus. In his preface Corneille explains that he does not have Nicanor married to Rodogune so that the twins might love her "sans choquer les spectateurs, qui eussent trouvé étrange cette passion pour la veuve de leur père." However, the difference between a fiancée's persuading a lover's sons to avenge him and a wife's doing the same for her husband is not so great, nor is the actual history so removed from the drama, that the threat of incest be totally absent. Cléopâtre's marriage to her husband's brother and Nicanor's engagement to the sister of Cléopâtre's oppressor reveal the suffocating quality of family relations as they do occur. Nonetheless, it is Antiochus's attachment to Cléopâtre which most dramatically threatens the organization of society. In its suggestion of an unresolved oedipal phase, this exaggerated bond points to a final dysfunction of Law. The child who accedes to the throne remains unable to separate himself from his mother. Failing to establish his own place within the power structure, Antiochus abuses his command through an excessive weakness.

The questions that Corneille poses here are complex. On the one hand, he shows the detrimental effects of a cruel maternity. On the other hand, Corneille points to a need for nurture, to a natural dependence, which neither Cléopâtre nor, as shall become apparent, Rodogune is able to satisfy. The political question is a woman's question. Shifting power out of the hands of men and into the hands of a mother, Corneille points to the psychic drama underlying the political tragedy. Psychoanalysis has taught us that the mother, as the child's first object of desire, must facilitate the child's entry into the symbolic. But why, Kristeva asks, should she want to aid this separation, since her own identity depends on her attachment to the male: "Si l'enfant peut servir d'indice à sa mère pour son authentification à elle, il n'y a guère de raison qu'elle lui serve d'intermédiaire afin qu'il s'autonomise et s'authentifie à son tour."[1]

Corneille does not glorify the cause of the women who refuse to serve the men. The women's sexual aggression to a large extent accounts for the corruption of the political model and the decline of absolutism. But if Corneille asks us to go beyond the elaborate pomp of the monarchy to a sinister reality, he is careful to suggest in the play's first scene that the dynamics of power are not of Cléopâtre's own making. Cléopâtre defends herself against a political system that had twice before subjugated her. The idea of her victimization is advanced through references to her suffering under Tryphon and to the people's refusal to recognize her authority:

> Voyant le Roi captif, la Reine désolée,
> Il crut pouvoir saisir la couronne ébranlée,
> Et le sort, favorable à son lâche attentat,
> Mit d'abord sous ses lois la moitié de l'Etat <...>
> Le peuple épouvanté, qui déjà dans son âme
> Ne suivait qu'à regret les ordres d'une femme,
> Voulut forcer la Reine à choisir un époux.
> Que pouvait-elle faire et seule et contre tous?
> (I, i, 31-50)

History—the lessons garnered through repetition—does not elevate man to a new understanding. Instead, it condemns him to know the horrific truth of his desire. In *Rodogune* man desires a woman who has been cut off from her origins as Earth Mother. She does not represent matriarchy, as this signifies an alternative to patriarchal corruption and oppression. Rather her femininity is a product of the political system that denies her fascination, refuses her difference. Cléopâtre, if she is to retain power, must subvert the established political structure. Significantly, the only possibilities for action presented by the drama are infanticide and murder of the twins' lover. Vengeance, although unpalatable, is Cléopâtre's only alternative to submission.[2]

Cléopâtre degrades executive power into mere vendetta.[3] Similarly, Rodogune's failed heroism hinges on an act of vengeance, sought through blackmail and murder. If her tragedy would appear less pronounced because she ultimately survives Cléopâtre to wed Antiochus, Rodogune's is nevertheless the more striking example of an inability to achieve heroic stature. Rodogune has a profound sense of the demands placed upon the hero, and, more than any other character, she attempts to live by these standards. Transgressions before an ideal held in such high esteem, however, ultimately precipitate a greater fall. Hence Rodogune's adoption of Cléopâtre's methods for vengeance makes her a more disappointing heroic model.[4]

Rodogune keeps secret her own preference for Antiochus until Act IV. Prepared to sacrifice love for honor, she devotes herself to avenging Nicanor's death. Marriage is for her the means to a principled end:

> De celui que je crains si je suis le partage,
> Je saurai l'accepter avec même visage.
> L'hymen me le rendra précieux à son tour,
> Et le devoir fera ce qu'aurait fait l'amour.
>   (I, v, 375-78)

Rather than escape to safety, Rodogune stays to fight for the throne. Her resistance, however, is explicitly connected to a sense of personal honor, to self-defense as well as to the defense of Nicanor. Her decision to use the twins against their mother follows Oronte's counsel that she protect herself from eventual humiliation:

> La Reine, qui surtout craint de vous voir régner,
> Vous donne ces terreurs pour vous faire éloigner,
> Et pour rompre un hymen qu'avec peine elle endure,
> Elle en veut à vous-même imputer la rupture.

> Elle obtiendra par vous le but de ses souhaits <...>
> Et le Roi, plus piqué contre vous que contre elle <...>
> *Vous laissera moquée*, et la Reine impunie.
> A ces honteux moyens gardez de recourir:
> C'est ici qu'il vous faut ou régner ou périr.
> > (III, ii, 805-18; emphasis mine)

Under these conditions Rodogune's self-defense is as legitimate, and actually complements, her defense of Nicanor. More subtle than Cléopâtre's because it is expressed as an ethical principle, Rodogune's desire for vengeance nevertheless constitutes the first echo of Cléopâtre's unheroic behavior. Rodogune's private emotions justify what she terms "ce lâche artifice" (III, iii, 843) whereby she exploits the twins' emotional ties to their mother. Like Cléopâtre, Rodogune demands that the brothers murder one love to safeguard another:

> J'aime les fils du Roi, je hais ceux de la Reine.
> Réglez-vous là-dessus, et sans plus me presser,
> Voyez auquel des deux vous voulez renoncer <...>
> Vous devez la punir, si vous la condamnez,
> Vous devez l'imiter, si vous la soutenez.
> > (III, iv, 1024-38)

Although it contrasts the political model, nature, as represented by the twins' crisis, is similarly deficient. Exposing the tendency within nature to stabilize, to deny all variation, the twins are unable to resist the rapid changes that occur within the political hierarchy. Their resemblance defines a passivity, an inability to survive the political imperative to distinguish oneself or be distinguished. "Tue ou meurs," this play orders, reversing *Le Cid*'s call to heroism.

Measured in the balanced antonyms of his speech, Antiochus's tragedy is a failure to see beyond the exclusive choice that Cléopâtre has imposed on him:

> Dans l'état où je suis, triste et plein de souci,
> Si j'espère beaucoup, je crains beaucoup aussi.
> Un seul mot aujourd'hui, maître de ma fortune,
> M'ôte ou donne à jamais le sceptre et Rodogune.
> > (I, ii, 73-76)

Antiochus's speech merely re-presents the horns of his dilemma.
Moreover, his sole effort to eclipse this pattern proves similarly ineffective.
Granting his brother brilliance, or public appeal, while reserving
preciousness, or private appeal, for himself, Antiochus would deny the
potential for one twin to be substituted for the other. He and his brother are
both assured satisfaction provided that they define satisfaction differently:

> Donc, pour moins hasarder, j'aime mieux moins prétendre;
> Et pour rompre le coup que mon cœur n'ose attendre,
> Lui cédant de deux biens le plus brillant aux yeux,
> M'assurer de celui qui m'est plus précieux.
>   (I, ii, 83-86)

Séleucus, however, completely deflates this notion through a proposition of
his own:

> Séleucus
> Vous, satisfait du trône, et moi de la Princesse.
>   Antiochus
> Hélas!
>   Séleucus
> Recevez-vous l'offre avec déplaisir?
>   Antiochus
> Pouvez-vous nommer offre une ardeur de choisir,
> Qui de la même main qui me cède un empire,
> M'arrache un bien plus grand, et le seul où j'aspire?
>   Séleucus
> Rodogune?
>   Antiochus
> Elle-même: ils en sont les témoins.
>   Séleucus
> Quoi? l'estimez-vous tant?
>   Antiochus
> Quoi? l'estimez-vous moins?
>   Séleucus
> Elle vaut bien un trône, il faut que je le die.
>   Antiochus
> Elle vaut à mes yeux tout ce qu'en a l'Asie.
>   Séleucus
> Vous l'aimez donc, mon frère?

Antiochus
Et vous l'aimez aussi.
(I, iii, 128-37)

The echoing of the twins' complaints, their near comedic imitation, reinforces their single identity. Indeed, the brothers' inability to distinguish between equality as a state of achieved balance and identity as the static balance of inaction causes them to seek solace in their own sameness. They fear all excess rather than see in this difference the potential for heroism:

Hélas! c'est le malheur que je crains aujourd'hui.
L'égalité, mon frère, en est le ferme appui,
C'en est le fondement, la liaison, le gage,
Et voyant d'un côté tomber tout l'avantage,
Avec juste raison je crains qu'entre nous deux
L'égalité rompue en rompe les doux nœuds,
Et que ce jour, fatal à l'heur de notre vie,
Jette sur l'un de nous trop de honte ou d'envie.
(I, ii, 109-16)

By Act IV Antiochus's particular use of the notion "entière équité" has still further implications. He points to a process of victimization that destroys, that is predicated upon death:

Exécutez son ordre, et hâtez-vous sur moi
De punir une reine et de venger un roi.
Mais quitte par ma mort d'un devoir si sévère,
Ecoutez-en un autre en faveur de mon frère.
De deux Princes unis à soupirer pour vous
Prenez l'un pour victime et l'autre pour époux.
Punissez un des fils des crimes de la mère,
Mais payez l'autre aussi des services du père,
Et laissez un exemple à la postérité
Et de rigueur entière et d'entière équité.
(IV, i, 1185-94)

Although this "rigor," new in the play, signals an act of heroism, a willingness to sacrifice, it seals this gesture within a series of events that act upon, or subdue the hero. That is, it defines a willingness to *be* sacrificed as well. Antiochus speaks the hero's part in expressing the need to strive

for equality. Still, he confirms the evil in nature by refusing to punish
Cléopâtre directly. He attempts to expiate his mother's sins through his
own suffering. Moving from the twins' stasis to their silence before
Cléopâtre and their subjection to her rule, the play now comes full circle
with Antiochus's acceptance of death, for this is the ultimate form of his
identification with his mother. Corneille has delineated the ineluctable limits
of a cycle, come to seem natural, that lacks the capacity for renewal. He has
structured a natural evolution that consumes Antiochus.

It is Cléopâtre who acts to resolve the crisis. She presides over the
scene of her death. Ritual is not a collective response but the final calculated
act of a character who has disavowed all ties with the community.
Manipulating the poisoned wine goblet, Cléopâtre transforms herself into a
sacrificial victim: *pharmakos*. In a confusion of ritual catharsis, however,
her act posits evil both on the side of the sacrificer and on that of the victim.
Consistent with Girard's model, Cléopâtre is effective in restoring order
because she is alienated from the community that still recognizes her as
being one of its own. Nevertheless, her assumption of the sacrificer's role
in turn reimplicates the collectivity.

Our vision is bifurcated as we watch the stage. Carried towards the
throne—"Approchez, mes enfants.../ Il est temps d'avancer ce qu'il faut
que je fasse" (V, iii, 1559; 1572)—and then away from it to the scene of the
crime—"Je l'ai trouvé, Seigneur, au bout de cette allée" (V, iv, 1611)—we
look to focus on the hero. Antiochus, however, merely returns our divided
gaze. He refuses every sign of the truth:

> Non, je n'écoute rien, et dans la mort d'un frère
> Je ne veux point juger entre vous et ma mère.
> Assassinez un fils, massacrez un époux,
> Je ne veux me garder ni d'elle, ni de vous.
> (V, iv, 1767-70)

The play ends with a puzzling sentence which calls into question the
restorative value of the sacrificial ritual that it has set in place. Vertical and
horizontal lines extend past the characters to the temple in the wings. The
focal point is actually a point of metamorphosis, a ritual that transforms
joyous celebration into the painful spectacle of mourning:

> Oronte, je ne sais, dans son funeste sort,
> Qui m'afflige le plus, ou sa vie, ou sa mort.

L'une et l'autre a pour moi des malheurs sans exemple:
Plaignez mon infortune. Et vous, allez au temple
Y changer l'allégresse en un deuil sans pareil,
La pompe nuptiale en funèbre appareil,
Et nous verrons après, par d'autres sacrifices,
Si les Dieux voudront être à nos vœux plus propices.

(1837-44)

Antiochus's sustained identification with Cléopâtre confirms, more-over, that her death offers society no final release from the violence that she has engendered. The beneficent act must be read against the maleficent act; marriage celebration must be understood to redouble funeral celebration: "N'importe: elle est ma mère, il faut la secourir" (1810). Sanction by Law is a contradiction, for Corneille represents the failure both of the individual to achieve an independent identity, and of Law to maintain a rigid distinction between the sacred and the profane. The vertical and horizontal lines of the play come together in an act of violence during which mother and son exchange roles without ever acknowledging their obliqueness to the Father.

The Aftermath of Crisis:
Héraclius, Œdipe, and the Legacy of Tyranny

Transgression is the hero's antidote for political and psychic repression. Mistaken identities and doubled roles lock the hero into a pattern of imitative behavior. Unable to distinguish himself, the hero reverts to a primitive identity of pure desire expressed through incest and parricide. Corneille's suppression of incestuous relations in *Rodogune* contrasts with his explicit treatment of this theme in *Héraclius,* where the potential for Héraclius's marriage to his sister Pulchérie constitutes the tragedy's major tension. The ultimate avoidance of their marriage distinguishes *Héraclius* from *Œdipe,* where incest is realized. Similarly, the twins' offense to their father in *Rodogune* is extended to the threat of parricide with the Martian/Phocus relation in *Héraclius,* and to the actual murder of Laïus in *Œdipe*.[5] Sequentially, the plays thus negate the capacity of ritual to contain violence. Ritual recurrences tend to demystify the process of representation and counter its effectiveness. Each tragedy confounds the moment of revelation by sacrificing the authority that society most reveres. *Rodogune* ends with the death of the matriarch; *Héraclius* with the death of the patriarch; and *Œdipe* with a poignant challenge to the gods.

All ritual activity depends on the sacrifice of one victim for another. And the selection of the king as the *pharmakos* whom society simultaneously condemns and sanctifies through the act of murder is no more the exception to literary than to social history.[6] According to Girard, the representation of difference is necessary to resolve the crisis. But Corneille inhibits the identification process by doubling the already doubled substitutions. In *Héraclius* the king once again is made the victim and an undistinguished hero comes to rule in his stead. In *Œdipe* the hero's blindness symbolizes the obscurity of his position to the gods. Combatting incest and parricide with suicide, he fights repression with repression in a struggle for independent recognition that is destined to fail. Indeed the comparison with Œdipe suggests the difficulty of distinguishing the hero from the monarch, the pure from the impure, even after the ritual cycle is complete.

A brief look at *Héraclius* and *Œdipe* confirms that *Rodogune*'s antiheroism is not a fleeting phase in Corneille's career. The later plays similarly insist that the hero cannot be considered a new guardian of the sacred. Rather than act to identify himself, he is identified by the community through activity that guarantees his dependence. Moreover, the hero extends the pattern of mimetic behavior even after the victim is named, thereby disharmonizing the ritual experience. Like *Rodogune, Héraclius* shows the hero to continue to see as the community has always seen, blinded by its former limitations. Paradoxically, Œdipe's blindness brings these limitations to light.

Héraclius's most striking feature—its exceptionally complicated plot—is the traditional explanation for its unpopularity. Héraclius and Martian both assume two false identities before becoming their actual selves in the resolving action. Léontine has substituted her son Léonce for Héraclius, whom Phocas wanted to kill. Léonce was killed in place of Héraclius whom, in a second substitution, Léontine exchanged for Phocas's son Martian. Phocas thus raised as his own son the son of the enemy whom he intended to kill, while Léontine raised his real son in place of her dead Léonce. Corneille self-consciously theorizes that he "ne craindr(a) point d'avancer que le sujet d'une belle tragédie doit n'être pas vraisemblable." This "Avertissement au lecteur" might be taken literally as a warning to the reader that the "beauty" of this play borders on an overwhelming obscurity:

> Je serais trop long si je voulais ici toucher le reste des incidents d'un poème si embarrassé, et me contenterai de vous avoir donné ces lumières, afin que vous en puissiez commencer la lecture avec moins d'obscurité. Vous vous souviendrez seulement qu'Héraclius passe pour Martian, fils de Phocas, et Martian pour Léonce, fils de Léontine, et qu'Héraclius sait qui il est et qui est ce faux Léonce, mais que le vrai Martian, Phocas ni Pulchérie, n'en savent rien, non plus que le reste des acteurs, hormis Léontine et sa fille Eudoxe.

Corneille's term "embarrassé" suggests clutter, a burden placed upon the reader/spectator. Hence the phrase "vous vous souviendrez seulement" is more properly taken as Corneille's acknowledgment that this intricate network of character relations is the troublesome minimum that one must master in order to follow the play. And if I have quoted Corneille's remark in full here, it is so that my reader, in addition to appreciating Corneille's elaborate design, may have a convenient reference. The drama's extreme parameter, or ultimate truth, is revealed through a letter from Maurice's wife that Léontine presents as evidence in the concluding scene. Completing information provided by a letter from Maurice which Martian ("cru Léonce") discovered in Act II, the final letter reinterprets an already reinterpreted scenario. Reversing the distribution of identities established through Maurice's letter ("Sous le nom de Léonce Héraclius respire" <II, v, 600>), Constantine writes that Léontine twice substituted the princes. The closing letter thus recycles information known to Héraclius at the outset into Léontine's now fully realized design.[7]

More complex than the events surrounding the twins' order of birth in *Rodogune,* the entanglements of *Héraclius* produce further negative consequences. In this tragedy where, as Stegmann observes, "all standards of certainty collapse,"[8] identity is provisionally denied as both an ontological fact and as a quality of distinction. Passive before exclusive options, the twins fail to distinguish themselves. Shifts in identity subject Héraclius and Martian to the diverse and often contradictory responsibilities of son/brother/lover as these lead to threats of parricide and incest. Héraclius and Martian are thus deprived of the very choice which the twins refuse.

Corneille is here concerned, to a far greater degree than in *Rodogune,* with problems inherent in nature. In *Héraclius* nature exerts its influence against the political hierarchy and not the reverse. Corneille is careful to insist that the political situation aggravates but does not itself produce the stasis within nature. The *deus ex machina* letter of Act II intrudes upon Léontine's plans. Moreover, as she explains, "la nature y forme un obstacle secret" (II, vii, 754). Even when Martian thinks he is Héraclius, he cannot kill the man whom he believes to be his father's murderer and who is actually his real father. Phocas's paternalism is similarly countered by a natural resistance. His efforts to legitimize the reign of his son by having him marry Pulchérie, like his decision in Act V to spare Héraclius on the same condition, would unwittingly join brother and sister and thus meet with Héraclius's staunch resistance.

Corneille's extended treatment of the theme which he deliberately suppressed in *Rodogune* is a further challenge to ritual order. The incest taboo functions here as society's ultimate defense against disintegration. It mediates the action, preventing a chaotic disruption of the natural order. Taboo ultimately staves off tragedy, yet it stands as the play's strongest indicator of the threat of danger. As long as doubt concerning identity persists (that is, as long as there exists the possibility of incest), the characters are unable to act. On the positive side, their paralysis is an assurance that the horror of incest will be avoided. On the negative side, however, inaction prevents the characters from determining a remedy for the situation. The threat of incest, the desire for vengeance, and the possibility of marriage between siblings remain problems without solutions. Although Héraclius finally would be Martian to spare this friend who once saved his life, and although Phocas would "associer l'un et l'autre à l'empire" (V, iii, 1724), their generosity is stifled by Phocas's insistence that this celebration end in what would be an incestuous marriage.

Lacking a constant identity, the characters not only risk their lives by becoming pawns in Phocas's political design but also fail to become themselves and to realize their full potential. The conspicuous absence of the father (Maurice) and the primacy of the substitute role of the "stepfather" Phocas indicates that the sexual dynamic which Corneille is to treat explicitly in *Œdipe* is already at work in *Héraclius.* Here the father figure who would condemn the child's desire for the mother fails to exercise his authority. Sexual transgression assumes the form of original sin. And this moral offense, indicating an inherent evil, or natural corruption, comes to determine political corruption. The father, in a perversion of his role in the oedipal triangle, unwittingly supports his son's incestuous involvement. He thereby condemns not only himself but his progeny to a reign of tyranny:

> Dans le fils d'un tyran l'odieuse naissance
> Mérite que l'erreur arrache l'innocence,
> Et que de quelque éclat qu'il se soit revêtu,
> Un crime qu'il ignore en souille la vertu.
> (II, iii, 573-76)

Léontine in this speech would permanently stain Phocas's honor so that Héraclius's natural right to rule may be respected. Yet, consistent with the tragedy's obscuring cycles, this natural order is itself the source of the threat of incest and the controversy surrounding the legitimate heir to the throne. Léontine seeks to right the question of legitimacy once and for all but bases her struggle in a natural world where the very concept of legitimacy is foreign. She succeeds only in perpetuating the cycle of ignorance that denies the hero his right to know and to distinguish himself.

Héraclius moves us through layers rather than across distances, but the effects are similarly obscuring. Martian recognizes in the revelation of his true identity another act of repression. Completion of the sacrifice requires that he assume his persona, or public title, as Phocas's enemy. He must wear a mask to hide his natural identity as son, for to do otherwise is to contradict the spirit of the celebration:

> Je ne m'oppose point à la commune joie,
> Mais souffrez des soupirs que la nature envoie.
> Quoique jamais Phocas n'ait mérité d'amour,
> Un fils ne peut moins rendre à qui l'a mis au jour:
> Ce n'est pas tout d'un coup qu'à ce titre on renonce.
> (V, vii, 1901-05)

Martian calls into question the entire concept of natural identity which the play's ceremony has sought to defend. Extending the nature versus history dialectic to signify the opposition between inherited traits and acquired knowledge, Martian objects that the successful resolution of the crisis actually requires him to reverse the teachings of the play. Indeed, political harmony depends on a valorization of the environmental, or historical, at the expense of the natural as these define a primordial attachment to the father. This is the lesson in repression which Héraclius teaches him. Demonstrating strange solicitude in a play where the revelation of real identity has been the only source of salvation, Héraclius advises Martian to assume his former persona and to be another:

> Donc, pour mieux l'oublier, soyez encor Léonce.
> Sous ce nom glorieux aimez ses ennemis,
> Et meure du tyran jusqu'au nom de son fils!
> (1906-08)

While this forgetting allows the completion of the ceremony, it reestablishes the tensions which originated the tragedy.[9] Although a beneficent ruler, Héraclius, no less than his evil predecessor Phocas, rules through suppression. The good ruler acts in place of God, and Corneille allows us to appreciate Héraclius's benevolence. Yet the play's final moment conflates the problematic, obscuring this uniquely favorable perspective of the monarchy. The monarchic paradigm cannot be dissociated from the ritual through which it is authenticated. A ruler's power depends on the ceremonial trappings which permit men to forget nature's truth and to establish a law that protects them from each other. Corneille represents the sacred as involving more than sacrifice, or the recognition of the need to place limits on desire as this constitutes a new truth. The sacred act imposes an "oubli" which, albeit magnanimous, makes it vulnerable to reexposure.

This is the very tension that *Œdipe* exploits. More than ignorance or avoidance of law, Œdipe's transgressions signify a challenge to the truth that law pretends. Corneille's introduction of Dircé into the Sophoclean legend redoubles the religious question in terms of the political hierarchy.[10] Though Corneille politicizes Sophocles's theme, he nevertheless retains the broader dimensions of the original tragedy. Both Œdipe and Dircé establish a historical context through references to rights and judgments. Yet here, as in *Héraclius,* the criteria for judgment break down, pointing to an order that supersedes the heroic, or monarchic. Once again Corneille presents this disintegration of the political model through incest. No longer a mere threat, however, incest is now experienced as a defiant attitude on the part of the Thésée/Dircé couple and as a consummated crime realized by Œdipe.[11]

Responding to the gods' demand for sacrifice and her own need to assuage her guilt, Dircé accepts to become the victim. It was, she reasons, her father's love for her that motivated his fatal journey:

> L'amour qu'il me portait eut sur lui tel pouvoir
> Qu'il voulut sur mon sort faire parler l'oracle <...>
> Hélas! sur le chemin il fut assassiné.
> Ainsi se vit pour moi son destin terminé,
> Ainsi j'en fus la cause.
> (II, iii, 646-55)

By submitting to sacrifice, moreover, Dircé finds a way to free herself from slavery to a people who disinherited her. The oracle thus becomes the source of inspiration through which the heroine would elevate herself not only above her own crime but also above the crime of Œdipe's usurpation. Dircé would transform the gods' scapegoat into a martyr. Hers, however, is an angry gesture that is unable to produce any real expiation:

> Leur devoir violé doit-il rompre le mien?
> Les exemples abjets de ces petites âmes
> Règlent-ils de leurs rois les glorieuses trames,
> Et quel fruit un grand cœur pourrait-il recueillir
> A recevoir du peuple un exemple à faillir?
> (II, iv, 686-90)

Profiting from subsequent elucidations of the oracle, Thésée would become Dircé's brother to safeguard their love. He can perhaps be said to transfer this desire from his mother to his sister, that is, to resolve his oedipal conflict through a surrogate love:

> Si je suis descendu jusqu'à vous abuser,
> Un juste désespoir m'aurait fait plus oser,
> Et l'amour, pour défendre une si chère vie,
> Peut faire vanité d'un peu de tromperie <...>
> Si l'on peut à l'oracle ajouter quelque foi,
> Ce fils a de sa main versé le sang du Roi,
> Et son ombre, en parlant de punir un grand crime,
> Dit assez que c'est lui qu'elle veut pour victime.
> (IV, i, 1271-94)

Although in Act II Dircé is quick to admonish Thésée about the need for heroic sacrifice, she eventually falters in her own ability to "n'aime(r) plus qu'en sœur" (1261), to abandon this incestuous love and defend her honor. Indeed, the play evolves to show Dircé and Thésée coming to terms with a world whose mystery continually eludes them. Counter to their expectations, they must watch the innocent action become crime. Counter to their intentions, they must witness a usurper king become a hero through his final challenge to the gods.

Œdipe's transgression responds to a sacrificial crisis as this defines a general breakdown of Law and the collapse of identities or system of differentiation. Yet the violence associated with Œdipe prevents the condensation of the play's signifiers into a unique sign of restoration. Corneille very deliberately rejects tragic catharsis for a political causality:

> ...j'ai rectifié ce qu'Aristote y trouve sans raison, et qu'il n'excuse que parce qu'il arrive avant le commencement de la pièce, et j'ai fait en sorte qu'Œdipe, loin de se croire l'auteur de la mort du Roi son prédécesseur, s'imagine l'avoir vengée sur trois brigands, à qui le bruit commun l'attribue, et ce n'est pas un petit artifice qu'il s'en convainque lui-même lorsqu'il en veut convaincre Phorbas.[12]

Corneille denies the hero's criminality in ascribing to him this motive. Œdipe is noble because he acts in defense of his father. Yet, in a further complication of the dynamics of the sacrifice, Corneille insists through Thésée that the real crime is an offense to the institution of monarchy:

> Le crime n'est pas grand s'il fut seul contre trois,
> Mais jamais sans forfait on ne se prend aux rois,
> Et fussent-ils cachés sous un habit champêtre,
> Leur propre majesté les doit faire connaître.
>   (IV, ii, 1347-50)

Ultimately, Œdipe accepts the truth of the oracle. His moment of revelation, however, is dulled by his accusation of the gods. Knowledge is literally a blind alley, an awareness that is a misperception with respect to both the past, where he was prevented from penetrating true identities, and the present, where he comes to know himself as other:

Aux crimes malgré moi l'ordre du ciel m'attache:
Pour m'y faire tomber à moi-même il me cache,
Il offre, en m'aveuglant sur ce qu'il a prédit,
Mon père à mon épée, et ma mère à mon lit.
(V, v, 1825-28)

Arguing against the traditional critical interpretation of Sophocles's *Oedipus,* Tobin Siebers points to hero's blindness as his "greatest misrecognition." Oedipus views himself through the community's eyes. In blinding himself he thus demonstrates his inability to see without the direction of those around him: "Signifying genuine blindness, this act of self-mutilation signals the complete submission of the one to the horrifying desires of the many."[13] Sieber's emphasis is apposite for Corneille's Œdipe as well, although this thesis must be modified to account for the French hero's resistance. Like Oedipus, Corneille's character accepts the identity that others give him. In this sense he, too, is committed to a final misrecognition which in heroic terms translates as lack of distinction—the failure of heroism itself. But Œdipe dies unresigned to his fate. Refusing to look back at the gods, he denies their fascination. Much like the Racinian heroines who are to follow him, Œdipe takes his own life in order to limit the power of the ritual that imposes his sacrifice.

Adding to the cycle of reciprocal acts of vengeance, Œdipe's self-immolation calls attention to the body as flesh that resists transubstantiation, to the impossibility of transcendence.

"Prévenons, a-t-il dit, l'injustice des Dieux,
Commençons à mourir avant qu'ils nous l'ordonnent,
Qu'ainsi que mes forfaits mes supplices étonnent.
Ne voyons plus le ciel après sa cruauté,
Pour nous venger de lui dédaignons sa clarté,
Refusons-lui nos yeux, et gardons quelque vie
Qui montre encore à tous quelle est sa tyrannie."
(V, ix, 1988-94)

In this "eye for an eye" vengeance there is a reciprocity that impedes the ritual process. The gods have made Œdipe "guilty like the others."[14] He in turn, by his singular act of heroism, accuses the gods of founding a system of differentiation. Blinding himself, Œdipe transforms ritual into a "mimesis of appropriation."[15] He assumes the image the gods would

assign to him. But he in turn gives their law its rightful name: tyranny.
Œdipe's revolt signals the emergence of the person from behind the mask in
a final shift in perspective from the sacred to the profane.[16]

Tradition holds that religion and politics come together in the figure
of the king. Moreover, the king is considered a fixed point of reference
both within the text and outside of it, for the dominant theory of perspective
holds that we view the performance from the king's central position.[17] Yet
this single *optique* fails to account for the evolution of Corneille's theater
from a defense of feudal values in the early plays to the tyranny of
absolutism in the last.[18] It conflicts, furthermore, with the decentering of
the monarchy that occurs as a result of ritual enactment in the three plays
discussed in this chapter. While these dramas were not conceived as a
trilogy, together they suggest a pivotal phase in Corneille's career, for they
unmask the ritual process and structure a movement away from restorative
violence. They force us to see through the imaginary, to pierce the depths
of the unconscious which has grown no more altruistic for being exposed.
Political repression and psychic oppression survive in the aftermath of
taboo.

In the plays written after *Œdipe,* attention shifts to a ruler who
governs through repeated acts of violence. "Le parricide," Suréna justly
observes, "a fait la moitié de nos Rois" (V, iii, 1640). Sacrifice is murder,
murder of the Father, and all its royal ceremony cannot transform this
destruction into "restorative violence." Indeed, *Suréna* suggests that
parricide has replaced ritual as law; for the outbreak of violence at the end of
the play offers society neither catharsis nor forgetting. Girard postulates
that ritual is effective only as long as the community remains ignorant of its
dynamics: "le religieux protège les hommes tant que son fondement ultime
n'est pas dévoilé. A débusquer le monstre de son ultime repaire, on risque
de le déchaîner à tout jamais."[19] Corneille's exposition of the monarchy's
"reign of terror," his introduction of a profane hero into a world whose
sanctity depends on a political pragmatism that demystifies itself, begins
with *Rodogune, Héraclius,* and *Œdipe.* The actions of these plays are so
complex that to understand them we must appreciate the mechanics of
substitution, and we therefore come to know the workings of the political
process. Capable of the sophistication required to identify the victim, we
are likewise capable of identifying the ritual that kills him. In Corneille's
theater the "fondement ultime" of tyranny is unveiled through the
designation process.[20]

The oedipal theme as studied here is more than a metaphor of transgression. To note the gradual reemergence of incest and parricide is not to condemn the theater to endless re-presentations of a unique drama. Because it occurs in sophisticated cultures with elaborate political systems, the collapse of taboo cannot be dissociated from the manipulation of events that implies a conscious awareness of the dynamics of power. What mystification and celebration do occur on Corneille's stage is the effect of the theater, which assumes the ritual reordering of events. Ceremony is not lost; rather it becomes the domain of the playwright. Corneille mirrors back to the king a likeness in which he recognizes himself, but in which he sees reflected more than he is accustomed to observe in his palace mirror.

Chapter Three

The Sacrilege of Suicide: Racine's Double-Edged Sword

RACINE'S PATRIARCHAL HISTORIOGRAPHY sees the extension of the past in the present. The suspension of time in one glorious moment of celebration is the result of three kinds of repetitions: 1. the global historic: duplication of events along the diachronic axis (for example, the instance of narration as a representation within a representation); 2. paradigmatic shifts: power extended through a male hierarchy; action which imitates an earlier action described in narrative; 3. the particular actions of characters who act out of devotion to a principle of fidelity. The latter suggest the confluence of art and politics: tragedy imitates a world whose Law is a command to imitate. All three points are connected in ritual enactment, but it is the third point which provides the most important focus for this activity. Points one and two shall be discussed in the following chapter.

Any ritual or system of rites functions to order history, to give shape to the otherwise meaningless succession of events that constitute lived experience. Ritual assimilates the specific historic moment into a culture or tradition that transcends it. As was the case for Corneille, ritual in Racine's theater is connected to both tragedy—a symmetrically perfect art form that represents a stable world, a society of known and complementary identities modeled after the Father—and the tragic, the experience of loss that tragedy produces. Whereas Corneille measures the hero's stature in terms of a competitive political model, Racine makes his hero fight for autonomy within a fixed social organization. Unlike Corneille's heroes who struggle to create a world for themselves, the Racinian hero inherits an old and inflexible society which he must fight to have his own voice heard. The complexity of this situation is reflected in the fact that Racine's depiction of a society in crisis—a sacrificial crisis, as Girard employs the term—reflects as much the danger avoided through ritual as the danger inflicted by it. While ritual is commonly understood to represent Law and the prohibition of transgression, it is arguably the case that in Racine's theater ritual enactment represents both the reinforcement and the transgression of Law. Exposing the violence done to the hero as society's crime against itself, Racine suggests the failure of ritual sacrifice to restore order more than provisionally. The sacrificial act is not synonymous with any real restoration but instead defines a uniform society whose violence is its very conformity.

Indeed, Racine presents a particularly complex example of ritual practice. Consistent with Girard's thesis, a lack of differentiation among society members provokes a sacrificial crisis, or sacrifice-ready situation. *Andromaque* denies the differences between men, *Iphigénie* between man and god, and *Phèdre* between parent and child as incest again becomes the focus of ritual enactment. Yet the resolution of the crisis depends on the reestablishment of identities according to a mimetic code that is a Law of indifferentiation. Sacrifice reaffirms a hierarchical social organization that joins the hero to the monarch and to God through acts of emulation. Broadly conceived in terms of a Law that assimilates history to a tradition of imitation, the completion of the sacrificial ritual represents the privileging not just of the prince but of the collectivity at the expense of the individual. Traditional societies, moreover, deprive themselves of the energy necessary for renewal—the creative potential which extends the act of repetition to a sign of regeneration—by demanding that the hero accept to model himself after the example of his predecessors.

Simply put, Racine's tragic enactment consists of the hero's revolt against authority and the containment of this revolt. The hero's tragedy is completed prior to the play's close, which is non-tragic in its restabilization of established patterns, its resolution of conflict through prescribed canon. Racine's tragedies are often arbitrarily resolved through respect for classical standards of *vraisemblance* rather than for the *vrai* as it extends from the drama's psychological intensity. The hero's sacrifice purges society of evil and eliminates the threat of anarchy. Yet the hero's sacrifice represents a loss for which the final manifestation of authority fails to compensate. Thésée's presence on stage following Phèdre's death is the most outstanding example of this beleaguered power. But Andromaque's final victory and Eriphile's sacrifice are likewise ends that challenge traditional authority. The tragic cannot be fully explained either as a threat to society posed by the heroine or as the heroine's personal loss and suffering. Rather the experience of tragedy is inherent in traditions which can maintain order only through demands of conformity. The sacrifice that preserves Law must also be understood, therefore, to impose on society the sacrifice of its most vital and creative force. The theater thus destabilizes the very sign that it celebrates as ritual.

Andromaque

The concept of tragedy has an interesting application to *Andromaque* because the play's end satisfactorily resolves the crisis plaguing the heroine. Andromaque seeks the freedom to save Astyanax and to remain faithful to Hector and the heritage that he defended. Engaging her in a struggle to preserve the institution of marriage and the glory of the Trojan people, Andromaque's commitment to Hector extends well beyond their private love. Rising from captive to queen, she supplants the Greek presence in Epire assured of her son's well-being, her own constancy, and the continuity of the Trojan culture. Yet the play is not a comedy. The final scene enacts not marriage vows but funeral rites. Andromaque performs the play's concluding ritual as a widow, not as a bride. Her last celebration pays homage to a tradition bereaved of its heroes. Though it orders history, Andromaque's reign promises no freedom beyond the limits of ritual sacrifice.

The viciousness of history is apparent in the play's cyclical design. The drama of Andromaque's successful efforts to honor Hector begins with Oreste's return to order and concludes with his derangement. The movement through which Andromaque overcomes her bereavement through which mourning becomes memory, or sustained presence—is framed by Oreste's decline into emptiness following his loss of Hermione. Each of the play's characters, moreover, is pursued by a love which he rejects in favor of a love which eludes him: Oreste loves Hermione who loves Pyrrhus who loves Andromaque who loves Hector who is dead.[1] The cycle formed through this series of interlocking triangles turns haltingly. We can picture the four principal characters arranged in a circle on the stage, each looking nervously back over his shoulder as he moves towards the body before him. What Oreste, Hermione, and Pyrrhus must recognize as they glance backwards is an obligation that binds Pyrrhus to Hermione and them all to the past. Andromaque sees a threat to the promise that ties her to Hector. Her past lies in the opposite direction from theirs, as history has brought the defeat of Troy by the Greeks. History, though, offers no smooth ordering of time. The Greek power that now rules Troy is challenged by Oreste, Hermione, and Pyrrhus, as well as by Andromaque.[2]

Ultimately, Andromaque assures the continuity of experience. She makes of history's losses a sacrifice vital to the survival of tradition. Andromaque sought, however, more than ritual coherence, more than an order predicated on sacrifice. She wanted to end the struggles which mark the course of history. Andromaque had intended one final act of violence—her suicide—to bring a lasting peace to Epire. Now Pyrrhus's assassination precludes the necessity of this act. With Pyrrhus's death Racine restricts Andromaque to the tragic or sacred realm; he opposes her to the secular world limiting Pyrrhus. Extending the play's dialectic through the resolving action, Racine denies the restorative value of the ritual it enacts. Oreste loses Hermione who loses Pyrrhus who loses Andromaque who, having lost Hector, becomes society's final sacrificial victim as she mourns the dead.

Barthes has observed that Racine denies all mediation in his transformation of myth into theater.[3] Although the conflict of Greece and Troy is resolved, although the *historic* contradiction is exhausted, the *tragic* contradiction persists. History opposes Hermione and Pyrrhus to Andromaque. Instead, tragedy restructures this dialectic to suggest, on the one hand, that Hermione and Andromaque are allied against Pyrrhus to the extent that they respect traditional law, and, on the other, that Andromaque and Pyrrhus both morally oppose Greek authority in Epire. These tragic contradictions can be shown to reflect a sexual difference, a dynamic opposition which undercuts the (historic) harmony of the play's close.

Hermione and Andromaque oppose Pyrrhus on the grounds that a promise is a sacred obligation to the past. Both women believe a vow to be ineluctably binding. Were Pyrrhus to honor his promise to marry Hermione, Andromaque would be free to honor her marriage vows to Hector. The women thus share a common interest which they defend through a common principle. Moreover, Hermione commits suicide and Andromaque is prepared to do likewise to protest Pyrrhus's revolt.[4] Pyrrhus defends the rights of the individual, not those of the collectivity; he fights *for* freedom and *against* sacrifice. If, however, Pyrrhus is an "enfant rebelle," his revolt does not have all the negative overtones of the "monstre naissant" whom he prefigures. In more obvious ways than Néron, Pyrrhus asserts a positive change. He seeks the resolution of old animosities: "Peut-on haïr sans cesse? et punit-on toujours?"[5] Consistent with the tragic ambivalences outlined above, Pyrrhus's death signals both the safeguarding of traditional authority and the sacrifice of new energy that would enable society to move beyond conflict, beyond a history determined through acts of violence.

Racine, however, eliminates Pyrrhus to spare Andromaque. She is the drama's tragic figure, and we must see in her accession to power a sacrifice worthy of a hero. The play invites an important contrast of the protection afforded Astyanax by Pyrrhus and the murder of an innocent child that results from Andromaque's own efforts to save her son.[6] Both Pyrrhus and Andromaque are motivated by personal interest. Pyrrhus, though he would be a stepfather to Astyanax, would be a lover first—the latter is a condition for the former.[7] Maternal instinct similarly explains Andromaque's action. Yet Andromaque's sacrifice of an innocent child is intended to point to her resourcefulness in dealing with the "ingénieux Ulysse" (I, i, 74). Conversely, Pyrrhus's defense of Astyanax is doubly condemned: the Greeks recognize a menace to their security; Andromaque sees a threat to the boy's devotion to his father.[8] Though he encourages tolerance of Pyrrhus, Racine argues through Andromaque's deception of Ulysse that the sacrifice of life is vital to the preservation of civilization. The moral act is that which sustains a culture and a heritage, whatever the cost to the individual. Andromaque's second deception—her promise to become Pyrrhus's wife—also involves the sacrifice of a life, her own this time. To intend suicide is to valorize fidelity—and, by extension, the past above all else.[9]

As a woman Andromaque is engaged by this principle (albeit actively engaged) in a passive role. She would give her own life for "le reste" of Troy because she regards her self as nonessential in the strict (and not necessarily pejorative) sense. She is a nurturer—she fosters the cultural essence which is transmitted through the male line. Evoking this distinction, the following pair of quotations suggests that Andromaque understands sacrifice to be inherent in her feminine function:

Hélas! pour la (ma foi) promettre est-elle encore à moi?
O cendres d'un époux! ô Troyens! ô mon père!
O mon fils! que tes jours coûtent cher à ta mère!
                              (III, viii, 1044-46)[10]

Il est du sang d'Hector, mais il en est le reste;
Et pour ce reste enfin j'ai moi-même, en un jour,
Sacrifié mon sang, ma haine et mon amour.
                              (IV, i, 1122-24)[11]

Andromaque's language separates out a formal, or functional, self
that defines her emotions and thus substantiates her being. The following
lines, an example of the technique that Spitzer labels "de-individualization,"
show Andromaque using pronouns and articles so as to combine an appeal
for recognition of her particular situation with an appeal for recognition of
the general principle that obliges Pyrrhus, son of her husband's murderer,
to renounce his love.[12] The emphasis is placed on situation and principle,
not on personal loss:

Captive, toujours triste, importune à moi-même,
Pouvez-vous souhaiter qu'Andromaque vous aime?
Quels charmes ont pour vous des yeux infortunés
Qu'à des pleurs éternels vous avez condamnés?
Non, non: d'un ennemi respecter la misère,
Sauver des malheureux, rendre un fils à sa mère,
De cent peuples pour lui combattre la rigueur,
Sans me faire payer son salut de mon cœur,
Malgré moi, s'il le faut, lui donner un asile;
Seigneur, voilà des soins dignes du fils d'Achille.
                              (I, iv, 301-10)

First-person references to herself alternate with third-person designations of
herself as the "Captive," "Andromaque," "des yeux infortunés," "un
ennemi," and "sa mère." The first three terms in this series objectify what
Andromaque is to Pyrrhus and what she is to Astyanax, respectively. Each
category stresses her formal role—"malgré moi" becomes a literal definition
of her purpose. There is certainly a personal emotion, a mother's fear,
expressed here. But Andromaque defends her personal interests through
the mediation of a formal "I." Her language asserts a functional role that in
turn authenticates her emotions.

In this Andromaque is very different from the other characters, including Hermione. In contrast to Andromaque's purposeful assumption of a sacrificial role, Hermione's total lack of strategy is manifest in her disoriented speech:

> Où suis-je? Qu'ai-je fait? Que dois-je faire encore?
> Quel transport me saisit? Quel chagrin me dévore?
> Errante et sans dessein, je cours dans ce palais.
> Ah! ne puis-je savoir si j'aime ou si je hais?
> (V, i, 1393-96)

Comparing Hermione's suicide to Andromaque's suicide, we are impressed by more than the fact that Hermione perpetrates what Andromaque can only imagine. Hermione's suicide is a final example of her inability to control or act upon events so that they conform to Law. Avenging herself against Pyrrhus, she deprives herself of what she most desires. Her suicide does little more than recognize this loss. Overwhelmed by Pyrrhus's death and her own responsibility for it, Hermione takes her own life in a moment of passionate abandon.

For Andromaque the question of suicide involves more than the defense of Law. She regards suicide as the sole means to save her son while maintaining her commitment to Hector. Her decision is not only logical but also innovative. She carefully weighs the two options available to her and determines a third course of action that effectively denies the need to choose. She thus sees beyond the existing, exclusive situation to a more comprehensive order.

Still, Andromaque can guarantee only her objective to remain faithful to Hector. Pyrrhus, it is true, has revealed himself to be a man of principles. Though we might denounce his radical politics, we cannot disclaim his sincerity towards Andromaque. Nevertheless, Pyrrhus has been moved to care for Astyanax out of love for Andromaque. It is possible that her death would invalidate the contract binding the couple, that is, that it would provoke Pyrrhus to avenge her deception by returning Astyanax to the Greeks.[13] If this is a risk that Andromaque fails to recognize, it is perhaps because she feels most strongly about preventing Pyrrhus from usurping her husband's place.[14]

Racine's resolution is stark. Completely at variance with the drama's predicted outcome, Andromaque's survival does not fit securely into any particular context.[15] We have the facts:

> Aux ordres d'Andromaque ici tout est soumis;
> Ils la traitent en reine, et nous comme ennemis.
> Andromaque elle-même, à Pyrrhus si rebelle,
> Lui rend tous les devoirs d'une veuve fidèle.
>   (V, v, 1587-90)

And we have the form: the cycle now completing another revolution. A second leader is mourned by his wife and country. The funeral ceremony is the repeated moment that defines a past; it marks the arrangement of linear time into a patterned existence that structures meaning.

Something, however, is being held in check here. Something, like Oreste's madness in the play's final moment, is being restrained. As the continuation of Pylade's speech above makes clear, there exists the threat of renewed violence:

> Commande qu'on le venge; et peut-être sur nous
> Veut venger Troie encore et son premier époux.
>   (1591-92)

Inherent in Andromaque's mourning, furthermore, is the sense of loss, if not of compromise, at her according Pyrrhus respect that was denied Hector.[16] Andromaque treats her captor like her lover because each was her husband. The act, devoid of love, becomes a solemn rite, a formal function that voids the self of its emotion.

Completing the drama's cycle of substitutions—the child for Astyanax, Astyanax for Hector,[17] Oreste's (failed) attempt to kill Pyrrhus for Hermione, Hermione's suicide for Andromaque's (intended) suicide, funeral celebration for marriage celebration—this final doubling of a widow's duty suggests a sacrificial ritual which, like the funeral rite itself, orders society.[18] Ritual is an act predicated upon renewed violence, not the preventive act described by Girard:

> L'entreprise rituelle vise à régler ce qui échappe à toute règle; elle
> cherche réellement à tirer de la violence fondatrice une espèce de
> *technique* de l'apaisement cathartique....Le rite est appelé à fonctionner
> en dehors des périodes de crise aiguë; il joue un rôle non pas
> curatif...mais préventif.[19]

Pyrrhus's death in fact constitutes another "crise aiguë." It is inextricably linked to a history of vengeful acts. Violence is not simply a possibility announced by Andromaque's assumption of power (Pylade's "peut-être") but a probability determined by society's traditional resort to vendetta. It is this violent tradition which Andromaque preserves by paying homage to Pyrrhus.

Andromaque's rise to power is as basic to the experience of tragedy as her initial suffering. Though she is Queen, she is as much victim as ruler, as much mourner as vanquisher of "le reste" of Troy. She rules not through her own efforts—she first sought exile, then death—but as a result of Pyrrhus's assassination. Although she assumes command, it is the passive command of a devoted servant of history and time; Andromaque survives and governs with modest dignity. If she has realized a moral and political victory and has brought at least a temporary peace to Epire, Andromaque has lost Pyrrhus and the opportunity to make her own destiny. She has been denied the chance to assume through suicide the active male role of historical agent. She has lost, in a word, the possibility of synthesis. Fidelity to the past *and* to a present distinct from that past, denial of sexual opposition and all that it implies for the organization of society and its potential for (pro)creation are now precluded. It is for this failed potential that Andromaque can be said to mourn as she watches over a history whose diachronic progression is foreign to her own cyclical nature.

Iphigénie en Aulide

> La seule chose qui nous console de nos misères est le divertissement, et cependant c'est la plus grande de nos misères.
>
> Pascal

Iphigénie at first appears to be a perfect illustration of Girard's model for sacrificial ritual. The correspondences are exact, right down to Eriphile's Oedipal roots. The play, however, presents ambivalences that cannot be explained away by the concept of restorative violence. Greek society in *Iphigénie* is in the throes of a conflict that is in every sense a crisis of identification. The oracle requires the Greeks to name a sacrificial victim.

Eriphile is that victim who comes to know herself through the act of sacrifice. Like Oedipus, Eriphile recognizes contentment to be incompatible with knowledge. And she, too, is "guilty like the others." Her opposition to the Greeks reflects their own defiance of the gods. Yet where their revolt takes the form of a nonaction, a refusal to meet the demands of the oracle, Eriphile's revolt is an act that subverts the law which it satisfies. That is, she redefines the context of the law so that the act which executes it is no longer effective in limiting her.

Strife among society's members disrupts the hierarchical organization of society. With the king crying out in anger against the gods, the officer defying his commander, the wife castigating her husband, and the child pleading with the parent to submit to these protests, the vertical chain of command shows signs of collapsing on itself:

Agamemnon
Non, tu ne mourras point; je n'y puis consentir.
(I, i, 40)

Achille
Les dieux sont de nos jours les maîtres souverains;
Mais, seigneur, notre gloire est dans nos propres mains.
(I, ii, 259-60)

Clytemnestre
Cruel! c'est à ces dieux que vous sacrifiez;
Et, loin de repousser le coup qu'on vous prépare,
Vous voulez vous en faire un mérite barbare.
(IV, iv, 1292-94)

Iphigénie
Mais à mon triste sort, vous le savez, seigneur,
Une mère, un amant, attachaient leur bonheur.
(IV, iv, 1211-12)

The father, unifying symbol of the religious order, the political structure, and the family unit, is here plagued by indecision. Emotionally torn between military obligations and devotion to Iphigénie, Agamemnon wavers to the point of finally testing the gods themselves:

Grands dieux! si votre haine
Persévère à vouloir l'arracher de mes mains,
Que peuvent devant vous tous les faibles humains!
Loin de la secourir, mon amitié l'opprime,
Je le sais; mais, grands dieux! une telle victime
Vaut bien que, confirmant vos rigoureuses lois,
Vous me la demandiez une seconde fois.
(IV, ix, 1462-68)

We see in this a radical departure from the myth of the horde described by Freud. The father's opposition to the sons' pleasure occurs here in the form of the gods' imposition of sacrifice on a people who have already accepted limits on desire. The fact that the horde is replaced by a rigorously stratified society suggests that, were it not for the fear of losing Iphigénie, the Greeks would accept the subjugation of one man's pleasure to those above him on the political ladder, the dependence of the woman's pleasure on the man's. All the family members not only desire that Iphigénie be spared but also recognize that authority over her should be regulated by the laws of marriage as these extend from the incest taboo: that is, they agree that Agamemnon should give Iphigénie to Achille. Sacrifice is thus superfluous to law. Agamemnon's urging that the gods again demand Iphigénie's sacrifice points to this imbalance. The ritual reordering of events itself produces chaos. Sacrifice is a purely symbolic act whose violence has no creative function.

Sacrifice is not, of course, the only uncivilized activity in the play. If the issue of Iphigénie's sacrifice sets Achille against Agamemnon, this revolt grows out of, and indeed because of a jealous rivalry between the two men.[20] The debate over Iphigénie creates a forum for the explosion of existing tensions; it is the catalyst for society's violent expression of desire. A comparison with Oedipus makes clear, however, that Eriphile's death fails to alleviate even this primitive tension. Oedipus's crime justifies law. It forces recognition of the need for taboo to prevent further violence. Conversely, Eriphile isolates the Greeks from the source of their aggression, from the very need to sacrifice, by substituting herself for Agamemnon in the love triangle with Achille and Iphigénie. In the end the Greeks regain possession of Iphigénie without having to acknowledge any responsibility for their transgressions. Eriphile diverts attention away from incestuous relations and the danger of one family member violating another towards the even more threatening issue of blasphemy, man's violation of the divine. And Eriphile's sacrifice serves only to exacerbate this religious question.

Girard's model would allow us to see in her sacrifice a substitute for reciprocal acts of violence within the Greek camp. In *Des Choses cachées depuis la fondation du monde* Girard states emphatically that society's conscious appreciation of ritual evolves slowly over time.[21] Racine, though, already conceptualizes this crisis and this ceremony. He removes the problem from the hands of the gods and places it squarely in the hands of men. More ornamental than functional, ceremony becomes an act of transparent magic that leaves unanswered the fundamental questions of man's understanding. Achille, in the lines quoted above, acknowledges no authority but his own. His force of character lies in his ability to recognize his misery. Yet such *grandeur* is divorced from any Pascalian leap of faith. Achille's revolt brings him beyond a personal destiny, outside his own ambitions in love and politics, into the crisis of a demystified universe. His is a transgression no longer able to be contained by ritual.

This is the crime for which Eriphile is made to answer. Foreign, orphaned, captive, and alone, she is clearly targeted for sacrifice by her difference. Her love for Achille allows society to rationalize its choice of a victim. But it is not a sufficient offense to counteract the effects of society members' own transgressions. The disproportion between the limited specificity of Eriphile's attempt to take Achille from Iphigénie—a desire that, once articulated, never becomes action—and the magnitude of Achille's revolt is too great to be offset by her eventual death.

Quite the contrary, in both love and death Eriphile continues Achille's process of demystification. Falling in love with her captor, she transforms his violation into a seduction: she violates the law of her capture by finding pleasure in it. The self-imposed torment of an impossible love thus enables her to avenge herself against those who deny her independence:

> Je n'accepte la main qu'elle (Iphigénie) m'a présentée
> Que pour m'armer contre elle, et, sans me découvrir,
> Traverser son bonheur que je ne puis souffrir.
> (II, i, 506-08)

Critics traditionally interpret Racinian love as the character's subjection to an overwhelming force. Eriphile, however, demonstrates a definite volition. She realizes here an act of self-determination that Phèdre will later repeat.

The act of sacrifice is subject to a comparable manipulation by Eriphile:

> Déjà pour la saisir Calchas lève le bras:
> "Arrête, a-t-elle dit, et ne m'approche pas.
> Le sang de ces héros dont tu me fais descendre
> Sans tes profanes mains saura bien se répandre."
> Furieuse, elle vole, et, sur l'autel prochain,
> Prend le sacré couteau, le plonge dans son sein.
>   (V, vi, 1771-76)

The sacrifice is a suicide. Although he would leave us with a final impression of a family reunited, an "auguste alliance" (1794) established between Agamemnon and Achille, and divine justice reaffirmed, Racine subverts the sacred sacrificial rite. Eriphile maintains that she has prevented the Greeks from becoming involved in the ritual experience. Even if we reverse her accusation to claim that this last offense merely reasserts her own profanity, we see that she has disrupted the ceremony, broken its spell. In point of fact no sacrifice occurs. Eriphile's suicide deprives the Greeks of the pleasure, what Girard would have the *necessary* pleasure, of purging themselves. Directing attention to a moment in time which she alone is responsible for creating, Eriphile makes the priest a powerless spectator of the act that he intended to perform. His transcendent word is silenced in Ulysse's narrative. Discourse becomes the exclusive domain of the military, its immanence a sign of man's resistance:

> A peine son sang coule et fait rougir la terre,
> Les dieux font sur l'autel entendre le tonnerre;
> Les vents agitent l'air d'heureux frémissements,
> Et la mer leur répond par ses mugissements;
> La rive au loin gémit, blanchissante d'écume;
> La flamme du bûcher d'elle-même s'allume;
> Le ciel brille d'éclairs, s'entrouvre, et parmi nous
> Jette une sainte horreur qui nous rassure tous.
> Le soldat étonné dit que dans une nue
> Jusque sur le bûcher Diane est descendue;
> Et croit que, s'élevant au travers de ses feux,
> Elle portait au ciel notre encens et nos vœux.
>   (1777-88)

Ulysse describes the coming of the winds in great detail so as to allow for the possibility of divine intervention. Nothing that he says, however, imposes this interpretation. In an illuminating study of ceremony in Racine, Jacques Scherer shows the playwright to offer consistently rational explanations for mystical occurrences. According to Scherer, the belief of a supernatural act in *Iphigénie*'s final scene is restricted to the "milieux populaires, habituellement tenus en piètre estime par la tragédie." Only the soldier sees Diane and "Racine lui laisse la responsabilité de cette assertion."[22] The conjunction *Et* before *croit* likewise suggests a possible discrepancy between the apparition the soldier thinks he sees and the actual event. Moreover, since the only substantive transfer of power during this scene is away from the Greeks to Eriphile, it is difficult to consider the gods' storm to be a consequence of the ceremony.[23]

Indeed, penetration of the oracle's truth involves more than the naming of the right victim, the identification of the signifier necessary to complete the sign. It requires an active understanding of the means of signification, an *interpretation* of the message it conveys. Calchas's gifts are limited to the first category. He translates the gods' language, impartially mediating their interaction with men. But the play also includes a judge, an observer whose tears censor the sacrifice:

> Tout s'empresse, tout part. La seule Iphigénie
> Dans ce commun bonheur pleure son ennemie.
> (1789-90)

The tears shed by Iphigénie do more than reaffirm her goodness. Identifying herself with Eriphile at the moment of her vengeance against the Greeks, Iphigénie mourns a personal loss. She views the sacrifice as a measure of the violence from which the others believe themselves to have secured a release. Iphigénie denies, in a word, Eriphile's role as scapegoat, as she-who-provides-escape. Iphigénie earlier appealed to her father for protection by emphasizing the pain that her death would inflict on her mother and lover. She now cries in silence, and her tears are the only transcendent sign in this demystified ceremony.

Phèdre

Phèdre is further testimony of the seriousness Racine accords this revolt against the sacred. Phèdre extends the transgressions committed by Eriphile: she experiences all the more scandalously a forbidden love as adultery and incest. Like Eriphile, Phèdre is an outsider; she enters the nuclear family through remarriage. Yet her status as queen assures the centrality of her revolt and its resolution through suicide. Phèdre's defiance of Law, moreover, has no counterpart in the form of an obedient Iphigénie. Hippolyte doubles Phèdre's role without providing any real alternative to it.

Again in this play we are made to feel the force of ritual because the tragedy is structured through acts of substitution and imitation. Phèdre would find Hippolyte in the labyrinth where Ariane discovered Thésée; Hippolyte would similarly defy his father by loving Aricie.[24] Hippolyte flees his hated stepmother while she remains in a politically volatile situation in order to be with him. But their opposite movements come together in a parallel series of denials, distortions, and confessions of their love. Indeed, as Mauron convincingly argues, Hippolyte's declaration of love to Aricie could be attributed to Phèdre "sans y changer un mot":

> Depuis près de six mois, honteux, désespéré,
> Portant partout le trait dont je suis déchiré,
> Contre vous, contre moi, vainement je m'éprouve:
> Présente, je vous fuis; absente je vous trouve;
> Dans le fond des forêts votre image me suit;
> La lumière du jour, les ombres de la nuit,
> Tout retrace à mes yeux les charmes que j'évite.
>   (II, ii, 539-45)[25]

Mauron points to still another source of identity in the fact that Hippolyte protests Phèdre's love only mildly.[26] In the scene of her confession, he quickly retreats from a burst of outrage, and he fails to name Phèdre's crime when later confronted by Thésée.[27] Within the context of this phantasm, Aricie functions as a substitute for Phèdre herself. The incestuous doubling of roles actually mirrors a reciprocally incestuous desire.

It is virtually impossible to cite the source of the violence resulting from this doubled, and therefore denied, identity, for both Phèdre's and Hippolyte's offenses to Thésée occur before the start of the play. Œnone's accusation of Hippolyte, Hippolyte's confession to Aricie (a blow to

Phèdre), Thésée's decision to send Hippolyte to his death (another blow to Phèdre) are reciprocal acts of vengeance that show no sign of abating. The scene of Thésée with Aricie following Hippolyte's death conveys a sense of the ravages produced by such violence. Hippolyte's forbidden lover becomes Thésée's daughter. This gesture is clearly intended as a sign of a renewed paternalism; it is an act of overt generosity meant to restore the family and to stabilize the political situation. It is not technically another oedipal drama in the making. Still, the fact that Thésée's adoption of Aricie, insofar as it is a substitute act, resembles Phèdre's actions towards Hippolyte and, as a political move, duplicates Hippolyte's own transgressions of Law shows the formal structures responsible for completing the drama to be identical to those which produced its tensions. Thésée avenges himself against Phèdre, whom he now believes to be responsible for his son's death, by protecting her rival. Moving into Thésée's home, Aricie fills not only the void left by Hippolyte but the space abandoned by Phèdre as well.

The play offers no final release from these reciprocal acts of violence. Identifying Phèdre's passion with Hippolyte's, Racine has made ineffectual the Law that condemns her; he blurs the line between good and evil. Transgression cannot, therefore, be understood simply as the characters' disregard for Law; it is the inevitable consequence of an order whose standards become confused by events. That is, transgression implies a shift from the singular order of ritual to a causal plurality, from a mechanistic control to the tragic. Guilty before Thésée, collaborators in a unique attempt to displace the father's authority, Phèdre and Hippolyte both deserve to be punished. Each dies, yet the play's many discrepancies preclude either death from providing catharsis: Hippolyte is guilty for loving Aricie but is killed for loving Phèdre; Thésée regrets his son's murder once he learns the truth about Phèdre; Thésée's satisfaction at Phèdre's death must therefore be equated with a desire for retaliation against the woman who cost him his son.

Moreover, the play provides two acts of sacrifice which must be read against each other. Hippolyte is an ineffective victim, a scapegoat who provides a model of negative violence. His death is mourned; his sacrifice is subsequently believed to have been misdirected. Girard's analysis of the scapegoat would explain this error as the failure of society members to recognize unanimously Hippolyte as the impurity who contaminates them.[28] It follows that if Phèdre were to have maintained her silence, Hippolyte's death would have provided a final release of tension. This very fact, however, exposes the tenuousness of the sacrificial rite, the volatile situation that is perpetrated when ceremony becomes a performance efficiently enacted in ignorance of the truth.

Phèdre is the second, surrogate, victim—*pharmakos*—whose death will end the violence of society's "sacrificial crisis." Phèdre, however, negates the principle of substitution upon which the sacrificial ritual is based. Her suicide is a calculated act of revelation that demystifies Hippolyte's murder. It does not compensate for the effects of the first sacrifice but instead extends its horrors:

> C'est moi qui, sur ce fils chaste et respectueux,
> Osai jeter un œil profane, incestueux.
> (V, vii, 1623-24)

Phèdre's insistence on the profane recalls Eriphile and the obstacle that her suicide presented to society's need for sacrifice. Indeed what Phèdre accomplishes in her last moments is a transfer of power away from those who wish to punish her. Taking her own life before the others take it from her, Phèdre dies, quite literally, with a vengeance:

> Non, Thésée, il faut rompre un injuste silence;
> Il faut à votre fils rendre son innocence:
> Il n'était point coupable.
> (1617-19)

Phèdre masterfully undermines Thésée's authority. Thwarting his efforts to stave off danger through an act of violence reserved as his unique privilege, she disproves the father's claim to protect society. Her admission of guilt frees her from the specificity of evil viewed through the father's eye. She judges and condemns herself, and in so doing transforms carnal desire into the pleasure of the incarnate word. Barthes aptly terms her confession a "coïncidence totale avec le fait, elle est *correction*."[29] Yet Phèdre radically alters the world that she leaves. Her confession is more a compensation than an adjustment back to a prior state. The purity she restores to society is that of knowledge, of knowing sacrifice to confound man's ability to regulate a desire finally understood to be real.

The concept of the *pharmakos,* therefore, while essential to the structure of Racine's tragedy, is not adequate to explain the play's many

layers of meaning. Even if one reads the play as an apology for
Jansenism—and I do not—the function of the confession as it grows out of
sacrificial ritual itself suggests the problem with making Phèdre the
scapegoat whose death reintegrates society. She is the victim of a divine
plan, but she is much more than that. Her death seals the social tragedy of
transgression—the fact of a mother's incestuous and adulterous love—as
well as the personal tragedy of the torment of this love. Kristeva's
perceptive study of abjection helps to sound these deeper resonances.[30]
Where the *pharmakos* is an object expelled by society, the abject—neither
subject nor object—survives ritual violence. The abject never ceases to
challenge its master, and this is precisely the tension that we note in
Racine's plays.

Kristeva encourages us to ask what are the merits of the symbolic
system for the characters in *Phèdre*. To pose this question is to assume that
the reinforcement of the social symbolic order depends not only on Phèdre's
confession as it expiates or purges society but—and this is the originality of
Kristeva's thesis—as it benefits Phèdre herself:

> ...le péché est ce qui s'absorbe—dans et par la parole. Par là même,
> l'abjection ne sera pas désignée comme telle, c'est-à-dire comme autre, à
> expulser, à séparer, mais comme le lieu le plus favorable à la
> communication: comme le point de bascule dans la spiritualité pure.
> La familiarité mystique avec l'abjection est source d'une jouissance
> infinie. On peut souligner l'économie masochiste de cette jouissance à
> condition de dire tout de suite que le mystique chrétien (comme le rêve,
> par exemple), loin de l'utiliser au service d'un pouvoir symbolique ou
> institutionnel, la déplace indéfiniment en un discours où le sujet se
> résorbe (est-ce la grâce?) dans la communication avec l'Autre et les
> autres...Source du mal, l'abjection confondue avec le péché devient la
> condition de la réconciliation, dans l'esprit, de la chair et de la loi.[31]

Phèdre is not a mystic. Her final moments on stage are, however, ecstatic
to the extent that they bring her through revelation to another world where
she achieves a final peace. Phèdre recognizes her destiny, in the classical
sense, and God's will, in the (neo) classical sense. The layering of Greek
and French perspectives is important to explain the evolution from the
sacrificial ritual to confession as this represents a turning away from the
singular needs of society, or the institution of the church, to those of the
individual. That is, even the fact of Phèdre's self-condemnation, when

taken out of the specifically pagan context of ritual sacrifice and placed in the Christian world of sin and pardon, points to a heroine whose death is a consummation both sexual and political. The ultimate value of confession is not the promise never to repeat the sin which society extracts from the sinner; it is the release for the individual who articulates the sin. Phèdre secures not grace from her father but the grace of having finally returned to him:

> Minos juge aux enfers tous les pâles humains.
> Ah! combien frémira son ombre épouvantée,
> Lorsqu'il verra sa fille à ses yeux présentéé,
> Contrainte d'avouer tant de forfaits divers,
> Et des crimes peut-être inconnus aux enfers!
> Que diras-tu, mon père, à ce spectacle horrible?
>   (IV, vi, 1280-85)

The feminine, Kristeva argues, is assimilated by the abject.[32] Phèdre here does affirm the dominance of the patriarchy. Yet Phèdre exposes the weaknesses of the men who control her life. Her language brings her beyond the limits of the Father's Law even as she affirms it. Phèdre has taken Hippolyte through the labyrinth and now makes certain that Thésée learns how they have relived the myth of his power. Speech allows Phèdre to penetrate the other side of the world enclosed by Thésée and to discover in the symbolic a sign of her own making. She experiences in language the will to power as a creative force.[33]

Ritual and theater separate from each other. Andromaque, Eriphile, and Phèdre represent a force beyond sacrifice, a potential for creativity that reflects back upon the limits of the patriarchal system itself. More than their transgressions, their losses represent a sustained threat to society's efforts to achieve harmony. Stability depends on a conservative ritual whose re-presentation is less inspiring and sustaining than the words of the heroines whom it excludes.

The following chapter looks more closely at women's language, for their speech conflates the opposition of the abject with the sacred-as-Law. Recounting her tragedy, the woman/abject opposes the sacred-as-Law with the sacred-as-art. Law comes finally to represent abjection as the woman tells her own history. In addition to the plays discussed in the present chapter, I will examine the Roman *Bérénice* and the biblical *Athalie* to establish how in the women's representations of history the notion of ceremony evolves from ritual to art. Beyond any autobiographical detail, the women's self-portraits provide a valuable commentary of the Law that requires their sacrifice. To look back is to look beyond the patriarchy's intolerance of difference and change. In these women's voices Racine's theater finds a response to the limits of ritual sacrifice. This is the art of retrospective.

Chapter Four

Retrospective on Racine

The Portrait

ANDROMAQUE, BERENICE, IPHIGENIE, Phèdre, and *Athalie* have in common that they inform our view of history through the perspective of the female characters. The plays' speeches are punctuated by important narratives delivered by the heroines. A representation within a representation, the narrative is a model for action that imitates the past. But the narrative does more than repeat, or ritualize, history. Faithful to objective reality, the women's accounts of the events befallen them stand nevertheless as a challenge to patriarchal rule.

The conflicting demands of historical narrative and personal revolt are managed through a technique which I shall call the *painting of self-interest (amour-propre)*, whereby the woman's protean, psychological self emerges within her ordered and hierarchical depiction of the power that oppresses her. Projecting desire onto the historic moment, the woman paints a self-portrait which, although not necessarily physically descriptive, reflects her presence in the scene. The predominant rhetorical strategy is designed to produce a series of mirrorings that extends the effects of patriarchal law. The latter assures, as the preceding chapters have demonstrated, that the father's power be established through an exclusive or exclusionary practice, namely, a command that he be imitated. Racine's heroines, however, thwart this order, this "mimetic law." Isolated elements in the narrative reveal the woman's emerging role in Racine's historiography to be independent of example.

Representation depends on the interplay of similar and dissimilar forms as these authenticate the subject. Mastery in portraiture implies a control of, or access to the subject's difference through an identifying likeness. Racine's female characters, though, must be identified by the narrative's irregular or inconsistent patterning, for a system of resemblances assures not only her political defeat but her limited presence in the text. From *Andromaque* to *Athalie* the heroine's opposition to patriarchal law culminates in her personal sacrifice. Reflecting the hierarchical structure of the court of Louis XIV as well as the Jansenist belief in predestination, Racine's depiction of a woman's unsuccessful revolt has fixed referents outside the drama. Yet Racine's heroines dominate the plays that bear their names. A study of their self-portraits indicates, moreover, that discordant elements in the representation produce a change in the status of the referent. It is not finally Law and the ideology supporting the woman's sacrifice which the text validates. Rather this Law and this ideology are destabilized by what shall be revealed to be the narrative's disproportionate representation of the heroine's role. By detailing the woman's provocative presence, Racine suggests that the representation of otherness is vital to cultural integrity. Law, in its persistent re-production of the same, in its exclusion of a woman's difference, denies the spiritual renewal which guarantees the sanctity of ritual. The woman's narrative that performs this difference, however, keeps the theater and this spirit alive.[1]

If it explains the fixed structures found there, resemblance— identity produced through analogic chains—does not account for the narrative entirely. Isolated details which are not subordinated to patterns of repetition show the sign to be only a tenuous union of signifier and signified. Meaning is not produced in accordance with the play's rigid classification system. Indeed, once the play's codes are revealed to be equivocal, history ceases to document and becomes instead a process of interpretation. The heroine is able to assert a dynamic presence in the very text that testifies to the defeat of her desire. By painting a woman's self-interest in the same space where the patriarchy imposes her absence, the narrative produces two important consequences for the reader/spectator. If we recognize the diegesis as a historical document of patriarchal domination, the effect of the woman's voice is to shift our sympathies away from this power. Psychologizing the narrative, the condemned woman requires that we interpret events so as to authenticate her tragedy. More significant is the fact that textual inconsistencies depict a breakdown in the encoding process. Dissimilar elements in the narrative effectively disarm the patriarchy, reversing the effects of Law. In drama where speech substitutes for action, decodification of the diegetic narrative is tantamount to a successful revolt, for it denies the recuperative function on which the Law is based.

All tragic figures in Racine's tragedies share in a revolt against the patriarchy. Yet the heroines make a dramatic contribution to the Idea of history by subverting the *doxa* which grounds a verisimilar representation. That is, the women disrupt the process through which art reinscribes received ideas about the representation of art in life.[2] According to Kristeva, the real measure of versimilitude is not truth but conventions that allow one to speak about the truth.[3] Implicit in this concept is a relation between a social norm, or ideology, and the particular appropriateness of a character's action. Gérard Genette explains that for an action to be considered verisimilar, it must correspond to society's fixed notion of acceptable behavior:

> ...ce qui subsiste, et qui définit le vraisemblable, c'est le principe formel de respect de la norme, c'est-à-dire l'existence d'un rapport d'implication entre la conduite particulière attribuée à tel personnage, et telle maxime générale implicite et reçue. Ce rapport d'implication fonctionne aussi comme un principe d'*explication:* le général détermine et donc explique le particulier, comprendre la conduite d'un personnage (par exemple), c'est pouvoir la référer à une maxime admise, et cette référence est reçue comme une remontée de l'effet à la cause....[4]

Yet in Racine's narratives the correspondence—what Nancy Miller appropriately calls the concordance[5]—of the implicit maxim (here, the Idea of history) and the characters' particular representation of history ceases to occur. Formal inconsistencies subvert the truth value of the model, revealing meaning to originate in individual consciousness. They return our attention to the discrepancy between verisimilitude and truth: conventionally held meanings are exposed as prescribed doctrine lacking any absolute truth value. Portraying an emerging self no longer contingent upon collective history, the women's narratives disclose more than conventions make probable. To interpret their texts is thus to know beyond the limits of mirrored desires.

A retrospective engages one in active reflection in order to achieve resolution. Racine's heroines look back so as to make their way through the confusion of history. But resolution, too, is an art. To resolve, according to Webster's definition, is to decide. It also means to progress from dissonance to consonance and to make distinguishable the individual parts of optical images or sources of light. These are the disparate techniques of narrative representation. Racine's narratives constitute history as the product of a thinking subject, of the I who, reflecting on the certainty of its existence, represents its own voice and its own image so that we take notice. The first part of this chapter studies *Andromaque, Bérénice,* and *Iphigénie* to focus on the effects of the woman's dissonant and dissimilar representation. Extending this analysis, the second part considers together *Phèdre* and *Athalie* to show how even fantasy, as part of the narrative art, becomes a formative element in the reconstruction of history. Racine's heroines do not change the history that happens to them, the fact of their repression. But they do constitute another power through their narrations: namely, the power of art to determine knowledge, their own power to judge and condemn the history that sacrifices them. So our retrospective, or reflection on the series of narratives which constitute a woman's place in Racine's theater, suggests that the playwright opposes history and culture not as fact and fiction but as the transmission of an inherited idea and its re-presentation so that knowledge is no longer certain. To look back is to resolve this difference: we hear the voice whose discordant sound history would silence and we recognize the presence of the creating subject within the history of ideas that excludes her. Our retrospective thus opens the enclosed space of the tragedy to the tragic influence of those who contradict its harmony.

The Narrative Art

> Dois-je les oublier, s'il ne s'en souvient plus?
> Dois-je oublier Hector privé de funérailles,
> Et traîné sans honneur autour de nos murailles?
> Dois-je oublier mon père à mes pieds renversé,
> Ensanglantant l'autel qu'il tenait embrassé?
> Songe, songe, Céphise, à cette nuit cruelle
> Qui fut pour tout un peuple une nuit éternelle;
> Figure-toi Pyrrhus, les yeux étincelants,
> Entrant à la lueur de nos palais brûlants,
> Sur tous mes frères morts se faisant un passage,
> Et, de sang tout couvert, échauffant le carnage;
> Songe aux cris des vainqueurs, songe aux cris des mourants,

Dans la flamme étouffés, sous le fer expirants;
Peins-toi dans ces horreurs Andromaque éperdue:
Voilà comme Pyrrhus vint s'offrir à ma vue,
Voilà par quels exploits il sut se couronner;
Enfin, voilà l'époux que tu me veux donner.
Non, je ne serai point complice de ses crimes;
Qu'il nous prenne, s'il veut, pour dernières victimes.
Tous mes ressentiments lui seraient asservis!
　　　(*Andromaque;* III, viii, 992-1011)

Andromaque's narrative is woven into an argument of protest. The questions posed in the first four lines are answered through the narrative, which serves as Andromaque's justification for refusing to marry Pyrrhus. Rhetoric is not ornamental but part of a defensive strategy. Beginning with "Songe, songe, Céphise, à cette nuit cruelle," and ending with "Voilà par quels exploits il sut se couronner," Andromaque's narrative tells the history of Troy's defeat by the Greeks. Although it culminates in her own capture by Pyrrhus, the narrative sustains a plea of protest. Against Pyrrhus Andromaque protects her loyalty to Hector, to Troy, and to the Law that is a promise to remember.

The tension of this speech results from the complex relation of the narrative to the theatrical moment of Andromaque's performance of it. The narrative does not respect the couplet divisions of the text. Its concluding line is rhymed after Andromaque returns to a discussion of the actual crisis: "Enfin, voilà l'époux que tu me veux donner." The narrative cannot, therefore, be considered a closed form; the history that it recounts is not yet complete.

Indeed, the open-ended history is announced by Andromaque's self-portrait. Whereas the rhymes of the other couplets double one image with a more exhaustive or consuming one, Andromaque's references to herself move from a projection of weakness to one of strength. In the narrative's first couplet "nuit cruelle" is extended to "nuit éternelle." Similarly, the scintillating brightness of "yeux étincelants" becomes the incendiary horror of "nos palais brûlants." A passage of dead brothers is further denigrated in the following line as carnage. These images are again doubled in the shift from "mourants" to "expirants," which also stresses the emptying of human life, the victimization of those whose dying cries sound in the night. Andromaque, however, describes herself first as lost ("éperdue"), then as possessing sight ("vue"), as this defines the power to recognize and identify. Bewilderment, the inability to master her fate, gives way to a discerning perspective as the master himself comes to seek her approval. By reversing the text's repeated patterns, Andromaque's self-portrait demonstrates the power that she acquires as a love object. She paints a picture that actually subverts the recuperative movement through which history would assimilate her. Andromaque does not escape from fact into fiction but rather restructures the fact so that it is perceived from a different point of view, from her own perspective. She challenges the patriarchy at its foundation, breaking the representation of even the Trojan fathers into memories lived in the present ("Dois-je oublier Hector privé de funerailles?...Dois-je oublier mon père à mes pieds renversé?...") and events narrated in the past ("Sur tous mes frères morts se faisant un passage"). Each shift from the present to the past signals a refusal to be an accomplice, an unwillingness to mold herself into the male hierarchy.

With the imperative "Peins-toi," Andromaque not only refers self-consciously to her own creative ability but also announces a strategic reversal. Abruptly changing her focus in the next line from herself to Pyrrhus, she forces a space in the text that causes us to pay more attention to the process of narration than to the events being narrated. "Voilà" announces a summary statement, a recapitulation of the scenes described above. Pyrrhus, however, appears here to be the object of "Andromaque éperdue." Subordinating the act of aggression to the act of narration, her speech represents the aggressor as a product of her vision, a consequence of her presence. Restructuring the scene so that what is repeated or imitated is no longer the same, she stands firm in the very moment that chronicles her loss and capture. Andromaque requires not only that we learn the account of her victimization but also that we supplement this reading with the emotion that history would destroy. For if to recount history means for the narrator to speak of her own repression, the act of reading or listening to this account requires that one provide those elements which substantiate her voice as it is reconstituted by the act of narrating.

> De cette nuit, Phénice, as-tu vu la splendeur?
> Tes yeux ne sont-ils pas tout pleins de sa grandeur?
> Ces flambeaux, ce bûcher, cette nuit enflammée,
> Ces aigles, ces faisceaux, ce peuple, cette armée,
> Cette foule de rois, ces consuls, ce sénat,
> Qui tous de mon amant empruntaient leur éclat;
> Cette pourpre, cet or, que rehaussait sa gloire,

Et ces lauriers encor témoins de sa victoire;
Tous ces yeux qu'on voyait venir de toutes parts
Confondre sur lui seul leurs avides regards;
Ce port majestueux, cette douce présence...
Ciel! avec quel respect et quelle complaisance
Tous les cœurs en secret l'assuraient de leur foi!
Parle: peut-on le voir sans penser, comme moi,
Qu'en quelque obscurité que le sort l'eût fait naître,
Le monde en le voyant eût reconnu son maître?
Mais, Phénice, où m'emporte un souvenir charmant?
(*Bérénice*; I, v, 301-17)

"Rome," Phénice has cautioned, "hait tous les rois, et Bérénice est reine" (296). In its faithful mirroring of the scene, the narrative sustains a view of Roman rule so absolute as to subordinate even the emperor. But if the sights and details that Bérénice enumerates are so many signs of the law that reads "l'hymen chez les Romains n'admet qu'une Romaine" (295), her imagination transforms these signs into a pleasant remembrance ("souvenir charmant"). To read the law is to read the law as Bérénice interprets it. Locating authority in her voice, we reject the authorial model that excludes her. Not fantasy merely, but discrete rhetorical structures influence our historical perspective. Bérénice renders a world more complex and heterogeneous than either her desire for Titus or Roman law would allow.

The narrative is doubly ordered through the insistent use of demonstrative adjectives and the recuperative "tous." These words echo throughout a text otherwise marked by the characters' silence ("Tous les cœurs en secret l'assuraient de leur foi"). They synthesize the diverse parade of kings, consuls, and senators into a unique paradigm of power. A spate of details assures representational accuracy: were Phénice to portray these events, she would do so similarly. Phénice, however, would not see in the world's recognition of its master the legitimation of Bérénice's history as Titus's mistress. Bérénice's art of persuasion benefits from the disturbing resonance of "Cette foule de rois" with "Rome hait tous les rois." Since the republic that tolerates no royalty now plays host to a crowd of kings, we might expect that similar dispensation be accorded Bérénice. While it is perfectly consistent politically to have foreign heads of state in attendance at the naming of a new leader, the contrast between Rome's declared hatred of all kings and their ceremonious presence in Rome makes the text vulnerable to doubled and even contradictory readings.

Paradoxically excluded and celebrated, the kings create the expectation that Bérénice, their female counterpart, likewise be present in this narrative which represents her probable rejection by Rome. Using the imperative form, Bérénice asks her interlocutor to speak so as to substantiate her presence. The questions which close the narrative similarly invite us to reread the text in order to discover there the person whose voice records and measures Rome's march before Titus.

Though Bérénice speaks from the vantage point of an observer, she does not assume the role of excluded individual that the events mean to assign her. She projects herself onto the celebration by referring to Titus as her lover ("mon amant"). More importantly, concealed along the surfaces of reflecting light that create the magnificent spectacle of the "nuit enflammée" is an isolated detail which assures Bérénice's pivotal function in this scene. The narrative establishes an opposition between those spectators who absorb Titus's light and those whose "avides regards" cast light upon him. The effect is not simply one of inverted images, of a further mirroring. "Et ses lauriers encor témoins de sa victoire" signals an important refocusing away from Titus as source of light, as an autonomous power, to Titus as object of law, that is, as Rome's loyal subject/victim. Insofar as *témoins* extends from *témoigner de,* this line continues the metaphor of perception. Yet the noun *témoins,* meaning *proofs* of victory, establishes the equivalence of signifier (*lauriers*) and signified (*victoire*). Such equivalences in turn suggest an opaqueness; the laurels obstruct the naming of Titus. Conspicuously, laurels are the only sign of victory in this passage not to be illumined. Moreover, Titus's success is rendered nonmetaphorically for the first time here as *victoire* substitutes for *splendeur, grandeur,* and *gloire.* The literalness of this description, its dependence on conventional associations, exposes the artifice of the light play above, and thus points to the conflict underlying Bérénice's speech. Certainly Bérénice is the most outstanding laurel of Titus's campaign, and the obstacle to his victory celebration. To the signs of victory that reflect back Titus's image is added another sign that gives off no light. Isolating the laurels, the narrative hints at the real stakes of Titus's nomination. Titus does not recognize Bérénice; he does not illumine the laurels or identify his love.

On one level Bérénice's description of Titus's return to Rome functions as a fiction, the expression of a desire that history will ultimately contradict. Still, the narrative stops short of a wish-fulfilling fantasy. The satisfaction of desire demands that Titus mirror back her love, that he, like Hippolyte, assume the role that history denies him. Bérénice obtains no such pleasure. Moreover, Bérénice's position away from the scene, like her speculations and her questions, reflects the tension that this moment held for her. In reference to the complex history that Bérénice creates, therefore, Titus's "douce présence" functions as an oxymoron rather than a simple metaphor of her love. Titus is both acquiescent and passive: Bérénice's sweet and gentle lover and Rome's sweet and conciliatory hero whose passivity determines Bérénice's loss. History cannot be interpreted except as a function of her role. Beyond any projected desire, this is the truth value of the text. Bérénice's narrative is performative, part of the history that she represents.

So if, in the end, Bérénice is defeated by law, she becomes its most powerful executor. Bérénice is Rome's victim, but she wins no small victory in adopting it with/for Titus. Accepting finally to live and to obey Titus's orders, Bérénice relinquishes Titus and forces him to abandon her. She asserts the authority that Titus and Rome would deny her. This is not a transcendence, as she herself suffers the cruel effects of the tragedy that she perpetuates, but a final stage in the history that they create together. She denies the male/female, active/passive, subject/object hierarchical opposi-tions on which the law is founded. Her narrative likewise refuses a perfunctory reinforcement of the powers of absolutism. Bérénice asserts her own identity from beneath the chain of signifiers that exclude her.

> Dans les cruelles mains par qui je fus ravie
> Je demeurai longtemps sans lumière et sans vie:
> Enfin mes tristes yeux cherchèrent la clarté;
> Et, me voyant presser d'un bras ensanglanté,
> Je frémissais, Doris, et d'un vainqueur sauvage
> Craignais de rencontrer l'effroyable visage.
> J'entrai dans son vaisseau, détestant sa fureur,
> Et toujours détournant ma vue avec horreur.
> Je le vis: son aspect n'avait rien de farouche;
> Je sentis le reproche expirer dans ma bouche;
> Je sentis contre moi mon cœur se déclarer;
> J'oubliai ma colère, et ne sus que pleurer.
> Je me laissai conduire à cet aimable guide.
> Je l'aimais à Lesbos, et je l'aime en Aulide.
> (*Iphigénie;* II, i, 489-502)

In this text which describes Eriphile's subjection first to Achille and then to love, we see emerge the lovers Eriphile and Achille. The couple is not constituted in any real sense, of course, but Eriphile's move from captive to captor is one of the definitive effects of her narrative. The text shifts from a literal description of her imprisonment to a declaration of love as it is rendered symbolically through images of violation and consenting desire. Moreover, the first and second parts of the narrative (lines 489-96 and 497-502 respectively) project very different images of both Eriphile and Achille. Eriphile's "I," heard only three times in the opening section, resounds seven times in the last five lines. The repetition of the first-person pronoun is reinforced in each line through an additional self-reference: "ma bouche," "moi mon cœur," "ma colère," "me laissai conduire," "et je l'aime en Aulide." Eriphile overcomes the deathlike experience of her capture through a narcissistic assertion of her self.

Her depiction of Achille is more intricate and reveals a sensitive control of the events that she describes. Before beginning her confession to Doris, Eriphile refers to Achille as a ravager:

> Ce destructeur fatal des tristes Lesbiens,
> Cet Achille, l'auteur de tes maux et des miens,
> Dont la sanglante main m'enleva prisonnière.
>   (471-73)

The bloodied hand is our only clue that the otherwise anonymous figure with a bloodied arm whom she describes in the body of the narrative is Achille. The metonymic shift from hand to arm indicates an increased violation. The repetition of the indefinite article ("d'un bras ensanglanté," "d'un vainqueur sauvage") and the fact that Eriphile dared not look at the face of her captor before entering the vessel create, if not doubt as to his identity, a space within language that cannot be made concordant with the identifying language of her male captor. In this space, as within the vessel that she describes, Eriphile assumes the posture of she-who-names, she who imposes her mark on history. Achille has become a neutral figure on whom Eriphile can project her love. The eventual extension of the hand to the arm is the mouth, the receptacle in which all reproach dies away. A metaphor for speech and desire, this "expiration" signals the final substitution. If, as noted in chapter three, Eriphile projects confident and deliberate action, it is because in her narrative a confession of defeat becomes a declaration of war and the vessel a vehicle of her own making:

Iphigénie en vain s'offre à me protéger,
Elle me tend une main prompte à me soulager:
Triste effet des fureurs dont je suis tourmentée,
Je n'accepte la main qu'elle m'a présentée
Que pour m'armer contre elle, et, sans me découvrir,
Traverser son bonheur que je ne puis souffrir.

(503-08)

This passage represents Racine's consummate rhetorical skill not only because of its explicative value within the play, but also because of its structural centrality for the entire corpus. Eriphile's narrative retains the story of capture from *Andromaque* and the reformation of the presence/absence hierarchical opposition so vital to *Bérénice*. At the same time it presages Phèdre's flight into the imaginary as an operant technique, sign of her control. It suggests, moreover, Athalie's emphatic "I" as she brings the history of Racine's theater to a close. Eriphile's narrative strategy is tantamount to a seduction and thus provides an important structural link to Bérénice's captivated glance at Titus and Phèdre's hypnotic response to Hippolyte. Fantasy is regulated by a purposeful and deliberate art of persuasion whose effectiveness depends on the subject's ability to penetrate the historical moment. *Phèdre* and *Athalie* represent Racine's most concentrated investigation into language as an instrument of persuasion. Narrating scenes of seduction, the heroines of these plays demonstrate the power of fiction to influence history.

The Seduction

The art of seduction represented in *Phèdre* and *Athalie* centers on recognition, on the knowledge of one's fate. The seduction begins with the mother's captivated gaze at the son. Phèdre's first view of Hippolyte, like Athalie's initial glimpse of Eliacin, are important moments which motivate the drama. In both plays the mother's ambivalence towards the son originates in this perception, yet in neither case does Racine present this scene to us directly. Instead, Phèdre and Athalie recount their experiences to other characters.[6] We may wonder why Racine insists that the mother's encounter with her son be described rather than enacted. Is this "performance of the description," itself a censoring device, one aspect of the seduction? An examination of the texts in fact shows that the characters do not imitate but selectively screen the events that they recall.[7] Phèdre's and Athalie's descriptions here are literally re-presentations, interpretations that reflect how differently each responds to the identical situation with the son:

> Mes yeux ne voyaient plus, je ne pouvais parler;
> Je sentis tout mon corps et transir et brûler:
> Je reconnus Vénus et ses feux redoutables.
> *(Phèdre;* I, iii, 275-77)

> Le grand-prêtre vers moi s'avance avec fureur:
> Pendant qu'il me parlait, ô surprise! ô terreur!
> J'ai vu ce même enfant dont je suis menacée,
> Tel qu'un songe effrayant l'a peint à ma pensée.
> *(Athalie;* II, v, 533-36)

The contrast of Phèdre's hysterical blindness with Athalie's frightened gaze, of the opaque with the transparent, suggests the ways in which Racine reorients this scene from one play to the other. Phèdre stands at a distance to herself, doubling herself in a representation which substitutes for that real world she can no longer see. Phèdre censors the real in order to experience the imaginary. Athalie censors the imaginary by identifying the real. The movement through which her dream informs reality is a discovery process that denies the power of the mind to perceive more than resemblances, to understand more than symmetry and proportion.

In *Athalie* Racine thus appears to revert to the pre-classical episteme. Throughout the Renaissance and the first part of the seventeenth century, knowledge was *divinatio,* the discovery of essences beneath the surface of things. Man sought the meaning of the plants, animals, and stones that God had put on earth. Language was an instrument for deciphering the truth, art the means to imitate the circular harmony that man discovered in the world.[8] *Athalie* is similarly concerned with decoding signs. To know is to uncover the truth, to identify Eliacin as Joas, son of God. *Phèdre,* on the other hand, typifies the classical preoccupation with signs that signify within knowledge, with the dispersion of the sign.[9] No longer concerned with penetrating the truth of signs as much as with understanding how one object was able to signify another, the classical period projected outwards, beyond the closed circle of the Renaissance. But if *Athalie* appears to react against this new freedom, this divinatory text is clearly not a sign of a reactionary Racine.

There is no reason to assume, anachronistically, that the revelations of this play are contained within the limits of the pre-classical episteme. While the characters' world is filled with signs that they must decode, the process of decoding shows that revelation is the vehicle through which Racine *subverts* the identification of signifier and signified. Specifically, our perceptions of the son of God are modified by the very speech acts that name him. Language is the means through which the drama produces as its end a change in our perceptions.[10] And the ultimate object of such re-presentation here is God. *Athalie* inverts the assumption that God first assigns meanings to things which man then discovers, suggesting instead that the characters' speech assigns meanings so as to censor God. The seduction that begins with the son will be shown to culminate with the Father.

We may find that such is indeed the case by tracing the seduction as it develops from *Phèdre* to *Athalie*. Phèdre narrates the fantasy of her seduction of Thésée in order to be united with Hippolyte. Substituting Hippolyte for Thésée and herself for Ariane, Phèdre recreates the myth of the labyrinth as a myth of sexual surrender:

> C'est moi, prince, c'est moi dont l'utile secours
> Vous eût du labyrinthe enseigné les détours.
> (II, v, 655-56)

While the letter of the text conveys Hippolyte's rejection of Phèdre's advances, its figures make him a partner in the seduction. His interpretation of Phèdre's intentions, his penetration of the ambivalences of her speech, constitute a response to the sexual act that Phèdre has initiated. The text does not rest with a discovery of concealed meaning but projects desire through signs that substitute for each other. Hippolyte's sword extends the arm that he will not raise, consummating the act that Phèdre would have be both an end to life and a satisfaction of physical relations:

> Au défaut de ton bras prête-moi ton épée;
> Donne.
> (710-11)

Meaning thus depends on the reinterpretation of similarities as identities. Phèdre insists upon the resemblance of Hippolyte to Thésée:

> Il avait votre port, vos yeux, votre langage;
> Cette noble pudeur colorait son visage.
>   (641-42)

Such similarities would simply connote an error in judgment, a false knowledge, if Phèdre were not able to structure another, more profound discourse beneath the mirroring of signs. If hope surfaces through Phèdre's guilt and shame, it is due to the spontaneous movement of her imagination. Extending her desire beyond the signs that restrict it—beyond the image of the father—she transforms law into scandal, repressed emotion into what Francesco Orlando terms the "verbal liberation of desire":

> De l'austère pudeur les bornes sont passées:
> J'ai déclaré ma honte aux yeux de mon vainqueur,
> Et l'espoir malgré moi s'est glissé dans mon cœur.
>   (III, i, 766-68)[11]

Phèdre cultivates the images of her waking dream until they give her satisfaction. Athalie, on the other hand, remains frustrated by the recurring image that haunts her sleep. Her dream structures an elaborate analogy through which history is shown to be ordered through reciprocal acts of vengeance. The horrific apparition of Jézabel in the first section of the passage is later explained by the image of the child that twice presents itself, suggesting that another mother will be killed by another son of God. The pre-classical belief that similarities root an infinite number of parallel relations along the chain of being is denied here, however, by the exclusive emphasis on the same, the already known. Man's link with God is precluded by resemblances that limit the space of the drama to the visible, to the actual history that it (re)enacts:

> Mais de ce souvenir mon âme possédée
> A *deux fois* en dormant *revu* la *même* idée;
> *Deux fois* mes tristes yeux se sont vu *retracer*
> Ce *même* enfant *toujours* tout prêt à me percer.
>   (II, v, 519-22; emphasis mine)

Although the dream permits Athalie to anticipate the events that it portrays, its redoubled terrors inscribe the word—*logos*—of God's oppressive law. Athalie is powerless to avoid the image that disturbs her sleep, powerless to do more than act out the history that it represents:

> Dans le temple des Juifs un instinct m'a poussée <...>
> Je l'ai vu: *son même air, son même habit de lin,*
> *Sa démarche, ses yeux,* et *tous ses traits* enfin,
> C'est lui-*même.*
>
> (527-39; emphasis mine)

We hear in these lines more than an echo of Phèdre's speech (quoted above). Although Athalie all but duplicates Phèdre's words to Hippolyte, she does not elicit from Eliacin a similar response. Phèdre's language is expansive, capable of reaching beyond the real and its strict opposition of father and son, law and transgression, into an imaginary world that permits one to be oneself and one's opposite, to proceed forward in stepping away. Athalie is unable to impose her will because she cannot effect this transformation. She is unable to create a situation in which she appears to the son as other than what he knows her to be. She fails, in a word, to seduce:

> Je prétends vous traiter comme mon propre fils.
> Comme votre fils!
>   Oui...Vous vous taisez?
>   Quel père
> Je quitterais! et pour...
>   Hé bien?
>   Pour quelle mère!
>   (II, vii, 698-700)

Athalie is not Phèdre; nor is *Athalie* generally considered to be an artistic achievement as great as *Phèdre*. Cook reminds us, however, that *Athalie* "is simplified, not simple"[12] in its structuring of ambivalences: "J'ai voulu voir; j'ai vu" (737), Athalie asserts upon leaving David's temple. But what has she seen? She believes that she has discovered Eliacin *and* an indication of the temple's treasure. The Jews of course know that Eliacin is Joas who *is* himself the temple's treasure. Exploiting this ambiguity, the final act plays on the literal sense of seduction as *détournement* (diverted attention), the antithesis of vision, clairvoyance:

> Te voilà, séducteur <...>
> Ce que tu m'as promis, songe à l'exécuter:
> Cet enfant, ce trésor qu'il faut qu'on me remette,
> Où sont-ils?
> Sur-le-champ tu seras satisfaite:
> Je te les vais montrer l'un et l'autre à la fois.
>   (V, v, 1705-17)

Athalie brands Joad *séducteur* when the doubled perception originates with her. Indeed, to Athalie this is not a deception but the ultimate truth. Although she must accept that Eliacin is Joas, Athalie vehemently maintains that Joas *is not* the temple's treasure:

> On verra de David l'héritier détestable
> Abolir tes honneurs, profaner ton autel,
> Et venger Athalie, Achab et Jézabel.
>   (V, vi, 1788-90)

Joad makes Athalie admit the power of his seduction, a feat never realized by Phèdre. Yet he is countered by Athalie, whose curse reaffirms the Jews' ties to her. Doubling the Jews' history with her own history, doubling Joas's investiture with prophecies of his corruption, Athalie continues to challenge the God who permits no other gods before Him, so that it is no longer clear who is seducing whom.

Thus far, the criteria for judging seduction have been broadly conceived as creating a scandal by allowing for possibilities where none is believed to exist. Both Phèdre and Athalie oppose the Father's singular Law. Joad, insisting that Athalie will be "satisfaite," intends neither knowledge nor pleasure but consummation as an exhaustion of physical energies, or death. We need to consider what in the characters' language is responsible for changing the structure of a given situation.

In her study of Molière's *Don Juan,* Shoshana Felman argues that the seducer's language is performative because it is self-referential. The result is the changed status of the referent:

Si le langage du performatif se réfère à lui-même, se produit lui-même
comme sa propre référence, cet effet de langage n'en fait pas moins acte,
acte qui excède le langage et modifie le réel: la sui-référentialité n'est ni
parfaitement symétrique ni exhaustivement spéculaire, mais produit un
excès référentiel, un excès à partir duquel le réel fait trace sur le sens.[13]

Language functions similarly in *Phèdre*. Telling Hippolyte "Oui,
prince, je languis, je brûle pour Thésée" (II, v, 634), Phèdre does not
identify the father. Rather, she imposes her will upon Thésée. Her
statement is not a lie but a promise to authenticate her emotion by
associating the son with the father. Hippolyte's supportive role during this
confession, like his refusal to condemn Phèdre when confronted by Thésée
in IV, ii, is an act of complicity that shows the balance to be shifted away
from the self-referential (illusion) to the referential (real).[14] The referent of
the signifier "Thésée"—now understood to be not a reflection of the real but
a (real) effect produced by language—is, as Phèdre intended, Hippolyte, the
father's challenger.

Joad's seduction is not posited in these terms. "Il est vrai," he
assures Abner, "de David un trésor est resté" (V, ii, 1649). Deceptive
because it recognizes but does not acknowledge Athalie's *détournement,*
Joad's speech nevertheless describes a verifiable reality. Once the
referential quality of the seduction is exposed, once the referent is indicated,
the constative "tu seras satisfaite" ("you will know the truth") becomes
performative. The speech act is a revelation:

> *Connais*-tu l'héritier du plus saint des monarques,
> Reine? de ton poignard *connais* du moins ces marques.
> *Voilà* ton roi, ton fils, le fils d'Ochosias.
> Peuples, et vous, Abner, *reconnaissez* Joas.
>   (V, v, 1719-22; emphasis mine)

This revelation is not apocalyptic. It prophesies nothing; it offers no vision
of a new world. Naming Joas, Joad identifies a preexistent reality. He
confirms the son's resemblance to the father. Structured through metaphors
that define difference in terms of the same, Phèdre's speech denies the
relations that exist between father and son. Joad affirms their identity by
insisting that Eliacin, Joas, son, king, and the temple's treasure all represent
God. This is a privileging of what Lacan labels the "paternal metaphor" in
which the signifier the "Name-of-the-Father" serves as a metaphor for the

symbolic.[15] In Lacan's system metaphor involves the substitution of one signifier for another that has its own signification. The substitute signifier acquires greater signification by compounding that of the signifier for which it substitutes. Lacan's analysis is pertinent because the symbolic order that he elaborates functions like the system of representation of the classical period. The *Logique de Port-Royal* establishes the potential for a signifying chain: "Quand on ne regarde un certain objet que comme en représentant un autre, l'idée qu'on en a est une idée de signe."[16] As a result of these similarities, we can interpret an inadequacy of the signifier within the Lacanian system as a sign of the inadequacy of the religious symbols that order the actions of *Athalie* into ritual, thus elucidating the particularly complex structures of Racine's text.

Although Joad accepts God's law and believes it to be his salvation, his language indicates that he understands this law to limit him. This is consistent with what psychoanalysis holds is the father's interference with the child's desire for the mother. In *Athalie* Joad is the father who separates the son from his mother and is this son who recognizes that access to the father requires that he renounce his own desire in the form of his son Zacharie, whom he must sacrifice.[17] The son's father elaborates a law that is vengeance:

> Par cette fin terrible, et due à ses forfaits,
> Apprenez, roi des Juifs, et n'oubliez jamais
> Que les rois dans le ciel ont un juge sévère,
> L'innocence un vengeur, et l'orphelin un père.
>   (V, viii, 1813-16)[18]

What is missing in terms of the Lacanian model is the repressed. Joad recognizes the act of revelation he performs to be the revelation of a real end, the renunciation of a desire for which there is no substitute.[19] It is most striking that Racine creates a situation that suggests the son's entry into the symbolic through language that undermines the primary symbol of the Father.

This reading discovers no optimism in Joad's final line. His emphasis on the justice of God's law does not allow us to conclude that the father himself now substitutes for the orphan son's desire. We hear the echoes of Athalie's curse that ring through this speech. Athalie has offered another version of "l'orphelin un père":

Fidèle au sang d'Achab, qu'il a reçu de moi,
Conforme à son aïeul, à son père semblable.
                    (V, vi, 1786-87)

Predicting what we know to be the biblical resolution of Joas's reign, Athalie's curse is performative of the same history as Joad's revelation. Her prophecy is an extended view of the same factual account that Joad offers. Each pronouncing the word *père,* Joad and Athalie appear to name the Truth, to say everything because the signifier refers beyond language (that which is signified) to the real. Racine implies, however, that the very Name-of-the-Father is itself a sort of death. The difference that the characters imply is (really) an illusion. Their respective versions of history, because they mirror each other, provide no hermeneutics. The signifier no longer signifies. Consistent with this disruption of metaphoric activity, the play's ceremony abruptly ends. Joas's investiture is completed before Joad's final speech about the orphan's father, and the choir, whose praises of God have ordered the play into a ritual observance, is now silenced. In this silence Joad's tribute to the father sounds insignificant.

Nor does the collapse of the classical system of representation as it occurs here indicate a final return to the pre-classical episteme. Similarity is not a form of knowledge but the occasion for error. The characters' discovery of likenesses in *Athalie* is deceptive, disappointing. The harmony of concentric circles that such relations were believed to structure in the Renaissance is replaced here by the cycle of reciprocal acts of violence that orders society:

Impitoyable Dieu, toi seul as tout conduit!
C'est toi qui, me flattant d'une vengeance aisée,
M'as vingt fois en un jour à moi-même opposée.
                    (1774-76)

Addressing the Jews' God, Athalie effectively denies what separates her from the Jews. The notion of being opposed to oneself in this instance further implies the denial of sexual difference. In this mirroring of male and female roles we see the failure to procreate, the loss of plenitude.

Mathan rightly, if indignantly, insists that Athalie is most a woman when she hesitates about Eliacin's fate:

Ce n'est plus cette reine éclairée, intrépide,
Elevée au-dessus de son sexe timide <...>
Elle flotte, elle hésite; en un mot, elle est femme.
                                    (III, iii, 871-76)

Athalie is feminine not because she is least assertive as a monarch, as
Mathan believes, or because she is most maternal, as Mauron contends.[20]
Rather, Athalie's hesitation is the only point at which, consistent with the
role of a woman who is both a queen and a mother, she rejects the precedent
of the men who acted before her.

   Adopting Eliacin, Athalie would protect the son whom she had
intended to kill. She would end her conflict with the Jews by refusing to
confront them. Although these ironies become apparent to her only at the
end of the play, the option that she proposes is of major importance. No
crimes are more heinous than infanticide and parricide. It is thus outrageous
that Athalie committed both in a single massacre intended as regicide. Yet
Athalie justifiably insists that she did not initiate the violence. The deaths of
her grandchildren are "rendered murder for murder, outrage for outrage"
(II, vii, 720) against the murders of her own family. How impressive,
therefore, is her move to escape this history, her instinct to bring Eliacin to
live with her. Recognizing separate powers and the practice of separate
religions, she would coexist with the Jews, not annihilate them. Her
gesture towards Joas is the only possibility that the play offers for ending
the reciprocal acts of violence, its only hope for a resolution that is not itself
an act of vengeance.

   In her final moment on stage, Athalie presents no alternative to
patriarchal authority. Yet in identifying herself with the Father, she
restructures the mother's role within the family and deprives the father of
his unique status. Thus, if the characters of *Athalie* have learned much
about deceptive appearances, they have learned even more about the process
of signification and the power of language to structure new meanings.
Exploding the traditional notion of *divinatio,* the mirrorings of this play
substitute a new history for the inherited Idea. Athalie and Joad have no
certainty of knowing because they exist only as reflections of each other. In
this space of this identity, in this very uncertainty, we recognize the power
of seduction. Here, as in *Phèdre,* Racine asks us to appreciate seduction as
the conquest of the other through the provocation of doubts and the
conquest of the self through the discovery that one has discovered no truth,
no law, and in the end no limit to desire.

The Other History

Considered together, the women's narratives recount another history, a history of the Father's displacement. Andromaque assumes the place vacated by her husband/king; Bérénice entraps her lover/emperor within the code of his own law; Eriphile acts for the priest who executes the gods' command, cutting a knife through their ceremony; Phèdre exchanges the son for the husband/father; and Athalie substitutes her curse for the divine Word. Yet it would be misleading to weave these narratives into a tapestry of matriarchal triumph. In the erotics of Racine's theater, women define their role through a confrontation with men.

Every theory of a subject, Irigaray argues, is appropriated to the masculine.[21] Sexual difference can be explained in terms of a unique male image:

> ...le désir du même, de l'identique à soi, de soi (comme) même, et encore du semblable, de l'alter ego, et pour tout dire de l'auto...et de l'homo...de l'homme domine l'économie de la représentation. La "différence sexuelle" est tributaire d'une problématique du même, elle est encore et toujours déterminée à l'intérieur du projet, de la projection, de la sphère de la représentation, du même.[22]

To apply this "problematics of the same" to Racine, however, is to assimilate sacrificial ritual to its performance on the stage, and this is precisely what the heroine's presence prevents us from doing. In the history regulated by ritual, woman represents evil. She is the heterogeneous element excluded from the patriarchy: death. But the heroine's narratives subvert the symmetry of the performance. Refusing the confluence of images in a unique likeness of the Father, Racine's female characters deny the very standards by which they are judged. So that if a woman's part in ritual guarantees a reproduction of the same (which for the man is the promise of an indefinite procreation), her commentary on this activity disrupts the patriarchy and precludes the indefinite extension of the paternal metaphor.

The mimetic system can sustain itself and develop only by exhausting a potential for reversibility; that is, through analogic shifts. While a woman's sacrifice completes the ritual cycle that sustains the paradigm, her self-portraits disalign it. Locating the focal point of interpretive discourse outside the Name-of-the-Father, the woman refuses metaphorical closure and shows the play's signs to constitute rather than to reveal Law. History is not the discovery of a predetermined order but the creation of this order. And signs made by men are subject to a women's reworking. Realizing as an effect of her representation her presence and power, the woman constitutes herself as a legitimate subject. Her narrative cannot be dismissed as fantasy because she uses her imagination to produce new knowledge, namely, the incompleteness and inaccuracy of official history.

       This chapter began with an analysis of mimetic and nonmimetic forms. I would like to suggest by way of conclusion that the latter be associated with an Oriental function because of the transforming effect that it exerts on the *doxa* that mimeticism presupposes. In the plays discussed in this chapter, only Bérénice and Athalie are Oriental in the strict "Near Eastern" sense, and Athalie represents more the Bible as a Western tradition than an Oriental geography. Nevertheless, all the women studied here represent otherness to a culture whose traditions assimilate history into a unique moment in time. The women are foreign; each suffers loss as a result of the patriarchy's denial of this identity. But the heroines' portraits disrupt the encoding process that documents their repression. They assert, in place of an abject, an Oriental: one whose status as other art recognizes positively. The Oriental function is political, certainly, but also aesthetic. It alone allows the intrusion of the nonconforming subject into a system of representation whose mimetic law systematically excludes it. Reading *Bajazet* against *Britannicus,* the following chapter explains how the Oriental play exposes the limits and vulnerabilities of the mimetic code for the creative process. *Bajazet* does more than expand the system of referents centered in Rome. It further illustrates an art of representing that precludes a uniform representation.

Chapter Five

Oriental Reflections: *Britannicus* and *Bajazet*

Racine's Orient

BARTHES HAS WRITTEN, ELEGIACALLY, of *Bérénice:*

> Tel est sans doute le sens de l'Orient bérénicien: un *éloignement* de la
> tragédie. Dans cet Orient se rassemblent toutes les images d'une vie
> soumise à la puissance la plus anti-tragique que soit: la permanence
> (solitude, ennui, soupir, errance, exil, éternité, servitude ou domination
> sans joie)...Quant à Bérénice, elle sait que, passé la tragédie, le temps
> n'est qu'une insignifiance infinie, dont la pluralité des mers n'est que le
> substitut spatial: rendue à la durée, la vie ne peut plus être un
> spectacle. Tel est en somme l'Orient bérénicien: la mort même du
> théâtre. Et sur les vaisseaux ancrés dans Ostie, avec Antiochus, c'est
> toute la tragédie que Titus envoie dans le néant oriental.[1]

Bajazet, however, is proof that *Bérénice* need not be read as a requiem for
the theater. Because in opening the very structures which guarantee tragedy
as a genre, the Orientalism after *Bérénice* does much to eliminate tragedy as
a signified. Indeed the "representational imperative" no longer is the king,
whose order has been exposed as a fiction, but the Orient, which literally reorients our perceptions so that we now see desire to be on a par with Law.

Contained in a unique dramatic gesture, part of a single tragic ritual,
Bajazet represents the struggle and defeat of desire common to all of
Racine's work. *Bajazet,* however, is not simply another European intrigue,
a *Britannicus* played in Oriental dress. It complements and complicates the
mimetic process through which experience becomes truth and memory. In
this chapter I will show that Orientalism functions as a vehicle for
reflexivity, thought mirrored back against itself.

Orientalism is a Western phenomenon which one needs to distinguish from the Orient itself. A branch of knowledge that dates back to the Middle Ages and reaches an artistic apogee in the nineteenth century, Orientalism is Europe's redefinition of itself through the broadening perspective of foreign culture. It is the filter through which the Far East is assimilated in Europe's own codes. As one of the constitutive elements of the classical episteme, the difference represented by the Orient of *Bajazet* is, then, a difference relative to the court of Louis XIV and not the authentication of Islam as an external, independent other.[2]

Bajazet's doubled structures and symmetrical patterning places it squarely within the Western mimetic tradition. Yet, as a result of reciprocal inversions explained below, *Bajazet* represents possibilities that *Britannicus* and the Roman model preclude. The exoticism of *Bajazet* provides a flight elsewhere, an escape from actuality. It does so, however, only to the extent that it (re)locates otherness within the French experience. We can infer from Pierre Martino's explanation of exoticism that the Orient appealed to the French because it offered alternatives which did not require them to leave France's shore:

> ...l'exotisme est surtout fait de ce sentiment de la diversité; il ne peut paraître que lorsque la pensée, enfin élargie, devient capable d'imaginer d'autres aspects que les paysages familiers, et de se figurer sur un autre modèle que les siens.[3]

The way in which this passage anchors difference in the self's own perceptions ("se figurer," "les siens") suggests that Orientalism was for the classical mind essentially a contemplative activity, an intellectual voyage into oneself. But if Martino's definition has the virtue of allowing us to shift the effects of the Orient away from the Orient itself, it ignores what those of us writing in the wake of Foucault recognize as diversity constructed through a unique representational model. The mimetic tradition is both infinite and plenitudinous, expansive and the source of its own diversity:

> A l'âge classique, rien n'est donné qui ne soit donné à la représentation; mais par le fait même, nul signe ne surgit, nulle parole ne s'énonce, aucun mot ou aucune proposition ne vise jamais aucun contenu si ce n'est par le jeu d'une représentation qui se met à distance de soi, se dédouble et se réfléchit en une autre représentation qui lui est équivalente. Les représentations ne s'enracinent pas dans un monde

auquel elles emprunteraient leur sens; elles s'ouvrent d'elles-mêmes sur
un espace qui leur est propre, et dont la nervure interne donne lieu au
sens.[4]

To understand the space exposed through the dispersion of the
indefinite Renaissance circle of resemblances, we need to look again at
Descartes's writings. In particular the *Discours* represents not only the
order of things, as Foucault analyzes it here and in the *Regulae,* but the
relation of the philosopher to his work. The *Discours* testifies to
Descartes's own presence in and impact upon the objective method that he
establishes. Read in this way, the *Discours* may serve as a model for
screening *Britannicus* and *Bajazet.* Descartes assumes the role of the first
reader of Racine's text, a text that his own investigations into the creating
subject have helped, if not Racine to write, certainly us to read. The image
of the meditating subject continues to re-present itself throughout the critical
process, revealing how representation intensifies the presence of the subject
within the culture that forms it.[5] Moreover, Descartes's representation of
this process enables him to reconceptualize both this culture and himself.
This is the West/East difference represented in *Britannicus* and *Bajazet.*

Descartes: Guide for an Intellectual Voyage

Giving structure to desire, Racine gives nature credence that reason
would deny. Cartesianism implies that the order of nature is concomitant
with the order of reason. Able to uncover the laws of nature, man is
similarly capable of determining the laws of reason. However, Descartes's
own representation in the *Discours* exhibits a persistent ambivalence that
belies the efficacy of the method itself. For Descartes diversity is synonymous with deception and error, yet the *Discours* is testimony of a circuitous
study and irregular application of the principle that it espouses.

Observing cultural variations throughout the world, Descartes began
his formulation of a method for elevating knowledge to the level of reason:

Il est vrai que, pendant que je ne faisais que considérer les mœurs des
autres hommes, je n'y trouvais guère de quoi m'assurer, et que j'y
remarquais quasi autant de diversité que j'avais fait auparavant entre les
opinions des philosophes. En sorte que le plus grand profit que j'en

retirais, était que, voyant plusieurs choses qui, bien qu'elles nous
semblent fort extravagantes et ridicules, ne laissent pas d'être
communément reçues et approuvées par d'autres grands peuples,
j'apprenais à ne rien croire trop fermement de ce qui ne m'avait été
persuadé que par l'exemple et par la coutume; et ainsi je me délivrais
peu à peu de beaucoup d'erreurs, qui peuvent offusquer notre lumière
naturelle, et nous rendre moins capables d'entendre raison.[6]

Drawing an analogy between books and the great book of the world,
Descartes explains that travel becomes beneficial only upon return to one's
native land, as this return home signifies a return to oneself:

Mais après que j'eus employé quelques années à étudier ainsi dans le
livre du monde, et à tâcher d'acquérir quelque expérience, je pris un jour
résolution d'étudier aussi en moi-même, et d'employer toutes les forces
de mon esprit à choisir les chemins que je devais suivre. Ce qui me
réussit beaucoup mieux, ce me semble, que si je ne me fusse jamais
éloigné, ni de mon pays, ni de mes livres. (pp. 10-11)

Presumably, the subject's retreat into himself is a departure point for the
discovery of truth as it exposes and contradicts the diversity of experience.
Yet the notion of reading, like that of modeling oneself after one's masters,
like the question of indigenous culture itself, is treated by Descartes with
great ambivalence. Having systematically criticized his own education and
rejected the example of his predecessors, Descartes turns again to his
heritage and to his books. With similar equivocation he argues, on the one
hand, that custom is the first source of reliable information and, on the
other, that custom is the potential source of misinformation:

...et depuis, en voyageant, ayant reconnu que tous ceux qui ont des
sentiments fort contraires aux nôtres, ne sont pas, pour cela, barbares ni
sauvages, mais que plusieurs usent, autant ou plus que nous, de
raison...en sorte que c'est bien plus la coutume et l'exemple qui nous
persuadent, qu'aucune connaissance certaine, et que *néanmoins la
pluralité des voix n'est pas une preuve qui vaille rien, pour les vérités
un peu malaisées à découvrir,* à cause qu'il est bien plus vraisemblable
qu'un homme seul les ait rencontrées que tout un peuple: je ne pouvais
choisir personne dont les opinions me semblassent devoir être préférées
à celles des autres, et je me trouvai comme contraint d'entreprendre moi-
même de me conduire. (p.16; emphasis mine)

The questions raised by Descartes concerning imitation have direct bearing on our reading of *Bajazet,* as we are the subjects who take the play's journey elsewhere and who must return home to evaluate what we have seen. This process is all the more complicated because the *Discours* imposes an important distinction between *representation* as the formulation of a method that ties the subject to history and culture and the *representation of representation* whereby the narrator calls attention to himself as a subject independent of both the method (this is the "I" of the autobiography) and history (this is the "I" of the Cogito).[7] Dalia Judovitz has noted that the subject's own representation is the condition of all representation:

> ...the subject, like space and time, is tied a priori into the structure of
> every representation. Hence the representation of the subject is a
> necessary part of every other representation because it constitutes the
> basis of all representation.[8]

The *Discours* indicates that the discovery of the universal subject (Cogito) through representation is counterbalanced by the knowledge that this (absolute) subjectivity is restricted by representation. Representation, as it overdetermines the subject, is offset by the representation of representation, which allows the subject to influence the world represented:

> ...je n'ai quasi jamais rencontré aucun censeur de mes opinions, qui ne
> me semblât ou moins rigoureux, ou moins équitable, que moi-même.
> (p. 69)[9]

It is precisely this distinction that I mean to pursue through a comparison of *Britannicus* and *Bajazet. Britannicus* elaborates a system of representation which the representation of the Orient in *Bajazet* exploits to the characters' advantage. Néron's passivity and Roxane's aggressivity will be measured against the lack of diversification in the Roman play and the successful diversification of the Oriental play. In the Roman tragedy we will find an illustration of Descartes's method as it limits the subject, while in the Oriental play we will discover a performance akin to Descartes's own representation of his representation of the method.

Centers of Power

> Socrate reprend ainsi l'opposition ma-
> jeure et décisive ...*mnèmè/hypomnesis*.
> Opposition subtile entre un savoir comme
> mémoire et un non-savoir comme
> remémoration, entre deux formes et deux
> moments de la répétition. Une répétition
> de vérité (*aletheia*) qui donne à voir et
> présente l'*eidos* ; et une répétition de mort
> et d'oubli (*lèthè*) qui voile et détourne
> parce qu'elle ne présente pas l'*eidos* mais
> re-présente la présentation, répète la
> répétition.
>
> Derrida, *La Pharmacie de Platon*

Britannicus and *Bajazet* depict two different forms of government and two seemingly antithetical struggles for control. Power in Rome depends on the denial and resistance of otherness. Néron fails because he would assert his difference, discover his autonomy. Inside the seraglio of *Bajazet* authority tends instead towards the assumption of otherness. To be polygamous is to experience plurality, the very option denied by *Britannicus*'s cyclical mirrorings.

Britannicus opposes power as both memory and remembrance with non-power, Derrida's *remémoration*. We discover two forms and two moments of repetition: repetition as life and desire; repetition as death and forgetting. The latter is blind and its path circular because it simply repeats the already-lived. It is ritual stripped of significance. The play requires that we distinguish tradition as cultural and political restoration from the automatic compliance with Law that is the son's imitation of the Father. Truth is inscribed within interpretive discourse and cannot be equated with the simple imitation of nature. This interpretive truth, or memory, however, exists in the play only as an ideal twice removed from the actual representation which juxtaposes non-power (repetition as death) and the power of the imagination (fantasy).

Burrhus elucidates what he would have the government's representation of an ideal that is imitation. The effort to actualize the ideal, to enact, as it were, the mimetic interpretation, is further complicated by the

fact that Burrhus presents us with an abstraction which is contradicted by
the action:

> Sur ses aïeux, sans doute, il n'a qu'à se régler;
> Pour bien faire, Néron n'a qu'à se ressembler.
> Heureux si ses vertus, l'une à l'autre enchaînées,
> Ramènent tous les ans ses premières années!
>
> (I, ii, 217-20)

Burrhus's efforts to mold history into a plenitudinous cycle of executive
acts is undercut by Agrippine's maniacal control of events. Exemplar of
remémoration, Agrippine respects the letter of the law only to obscure its
meaning. She profits from ambiguities that she herself creates by respecting
a chain of signifiers whose signifieds she all but ignores. Taking control of
her son as she has done before with her husband, Agrippine substitutes
propagation for maternity, control for nurture, and self-interest for
solicitude, all in the name of a paradigmatic coherence:

> Et moi qui sur le trône ai suivi mes ancêtres,
> Moi, fille, femme, sœur et mère de vos maîtres!
> Que prétendez-vous donc? Pensez-vous que ma voix
> Ait fait un empereur pour m'en imposer trois?
>
> (155-58)

The stages of femininity that she elucidates here root the mimetic enterprise
in narcissism, which is the source of the play's tension. Insofar as it
defines not only a legal code but a commitment to the values implied by that
code (i.e. a commitment to culture), the system requires individuals to
recognize needs other that their own. Ruled instead by self-love, all the
characters with the exception of Junie degrade the exercise of authority into
opportunism and personal aggrandizement.

No character exemplifies this lack of commitment better than
Narcisse, whose name gives an allegorical dimension to the play's
mimeticism. But if Narcisse's Machiavellian counsel extends the paradigm
of Agrippine's manipulations still further, it is Néron's more anguished
resistance to such efforts that brings the action beyond history to fantasy,
outside the limits of the classical model into the expansive world which
Doubrovsky appropriately labels the other scene of desire.[10]

When psychoanalysis speaks of imitation within the oedipal triangle, it refers to the mother as another subject. The father is Law, whereas the mother is the object of the child's desire. The child's needs for survival and his mimetic behavior both connect in the mother: she is the first object of desire and of signification.[11] Considerably older than a child at the oedipal stage of development, Néron remains trapped within desire's triangular form as adult life has complicated it. He lives this experience of separation from his mother as a moment of tremendous anxiety. Not only, as is typical of even healthy children, does Agrippine appear a source of anguish for Néron because he must fashion his self-image across the divide that separates himself from his mother but, since she would imitate the father, he must reject the very difference and identity created through imitation. He must, in a word, reject Law itself:

> Eloigné de ses yeux, j'ordonne, je menace,
> J'écoute vos conseils, j'ose les approuver;
> Je m'excite contre elle, et tâche à la braver;
> Mais, je t'expose ici mon âme toute nue,
> Sitôt que mon malheur me ramène à sa vue,
> Soit que je n'ose encor démentir le pouvoir
> De ses yeux où j'ai lu si longtemps mon devoir;
> Soit qu'à tant de bienfaits ma mémoire fidèle
> Lui soumette en secret tout ce que je tiens d'elle;
> Mais enfin mes efforts ne me servent de rien:
> Mon génie étonné tremble devant le sien.
>   (II, ii, 496-506)

Agrippine reduces Burrhus's cycle to the single reflection of the self's own image. Néron exposes this paradigm to be pure tautology. He resists the corruption of form by form, the automatic re-presentation of the same. In his hands history becomes a challenge to imitation, a threat to the power that requires the individual to sacrifice political initiative and personal desire. The genius he covets is the antithesis of mimesis; it is the freedom to create anew.

Where *Britannicus* extends the idea of mimesis to its logical and tenuous extreme, *Bajazet* takes this extreme and makes it logical. Although portrayed as a microcosm of the world governed by Amurat, the enclosed space of the seraglio is a world of contrasts that clashes with the rigid coherence of the patriarchy.[12] The characters deceive each other about the deceptions that they agree to commit together. And herein lies the play's coherence. Against the Roman logic that one thing cannot be both itself and its opposite comes the Oriental accommodation of mutually exclusive conditions. The tautological repetitions of *Britannicus* dissolve in *Bajazet*'s doubled truths. Acomat, in the name of power, and Roxane, in the name of love, undertake a plot against Amurat. Love shapes, or extends, the political struggle by acts of imitation. Yet the characters' reciprocal exchange produces a final transformation: Roxane subjugates Acomat's will to her own. Likewise, Roxane's use of Atalide to mediate her relation with Bajazet exposes both Atalide's central position to the drama and the mutual dependency of the three partners in forming a viable resolution. Roxane's pleasure with Bajazet does not exclude but, on the contrary, requires the union of Bajazet and Atalide and vice versa. Within the seraglio the status of all play and of all objects is double.

Roxane discovers her passion in Bajazet's love for Atalide. Still, her success depends on a choice experienced as a non-choice. Roxane vacillates between fidelity to Amurat and independence in the form of fidelity to his brother. With Amurat Roxane enjoys all the power available to a woman except—and this is a crucial exception—the status accorded a wife. The drama eventually dispels the very notion of a feminine power. Amurat controls the action even in his absence: he seals Roxane's fate from afar. This platitude defines the compromise of Roxane's love for Bajazet. With Bajazet Roxane realizes a vengeance against the authority that she would have her own. She experiences the impure there where she would enjoy the pure, the part where she would take pleasure in the whole.

Similarly, Bajazet hesitates between a principle of fidelity and political exigencies which force him to depart from the heroic model. The grievousness of Roxane's offense is compounded by Acomat's counsel to Bajazet that the offense be ignored:

> Ne rougissez point: le sang des Ottomans
> Ne doit point en esclave obéir aux serments.
> Consultez ces héros que le droit de la guerre
> Mena victorieux jusqu'au bout de la terre:
> Libres dans leur victoire, et maîtres de leur foi,
> L'intérêt de l'état fut leur unique loi,
> Et d'un trône si saint la moitié n'est fondée
> Que sur la foi promise et rarement gardée.
> (II, iii, 643-50)

Sounding much like Narcisse in his espousal of self-interest, Acomat nevertheless presents an important departure from tradition. Both counselors cite historical precedents. Narcisse's insistence on the right to divorce, however, is an argument for law:

> Auguste, votre aïeul, soupirait pour Livie;
> Par un double divorce ils s'unirent tous deux.
>   (II, ii, 476-77)

Conversely, Amurat argues against the very notion of contract which founds this law. Even the decision to separate, when mutually agreed upon, constitutes a promise. Like the marriage vow, the divorce decree is a binding relation, an extension of the mimetic law. Narcisse's statement thus contrasts markedly with Amurat's model, which illustrates the (French) belief that respect for law came belatedly to the Orient with the teachings of fidelity by Mohammed's followers.[13]

Though Bajazet is able to resist Acomat's reasoning, he is eventually persuaded by Atalide, who threatens to commit suicide if Bajazet does not act to save himself. She would teach Bajazet by her own example, yet the act of imitation that she proposes constitutes a sharing of partners rather than an exchange:

> Seigneur, vous pourriez vivre, et ne me point trahir.
>   (II, v, 727)

Atalide does not herself realize the full impact of what she proposes until later when, overwhelmed by jealousy, she reproaches Bajazet for yielding to Roxane. Still, a partitioning of loyalties is the only solution upon which the characters can agree, their only hope for avoiding suppression under Amurat.[14]

I will return below to the critical issue of the quality of Amurat's reign. It must be emphasized that polygamy within the seraglio does more than provide contrast for the Western way of life. At issue here is the relation of the individual to history. Indeed, memory as it signifies reason is challenged by the plural solution represented in *Bajazet*. However reluctantly, however inconsistently, Bajazet introduces a new historical stance by his decision to yield to Roxane. Faithful to the example of the past insofar as it repeats the duplicitous behavior of former leaders—to the extent that the model is inconsistent—Bajazet's compromise nevertheless signals an important innovation. Attempting to please one woman in order to secure pleasure with another, Bajazet proposes not the traditional renouncement of a promise but respect for this promise *in order* to protect his love for Atalide.

Unlike Néron, whose revolt constitutes a denial of the past, a rejection of the mnemonic screen which filters experience into a single paradigm, Roxane and Bajazet retain the memory intact while reliving it as something other. The projected union of Bajazet and Roxane maintains distinctions between opposites (fidelity/infidelity), although the notion of singular repetition is invalidated by the mimetic process. Mirror images authenticate imitation as the truth of that which is and is not, that is, as that which is not unique.[15]

This specular play is entirely consistent with the classical propensity for litotes. We have seen, however, that while the affirmation ("I love you") occurs for both Roxane and Bajazet as the negation of its opposite ("I don't love Amurat/Roxane"), the negation does not move the characters away from the love negated to the love affirmed. Instead it locks the characters between two loves as between two moments that history would make one. Thus while there are points at which, consistent with psychoanalytic theory, negation is the expression of desire, the characters' efforts to control desire are more complex than even this irony would allow.[16]

Fictions Within the Plays

Néron's fantasy occurs as the extension of an historical narrative.[17] Indeed, though it situates Junie's capture within a real time frame, Néron's detailed account of his reaction to this event is merely a prelude to the fantasy itself. Announced as a rupture, a revolution in time, the historical narrative prepares a break from the exclusive mimetic law to the original fullness of desire:

> Depuis un moment, mais pour toute ma vie.
> J'aime, que dis-je, aimer? j'idolâtre Junie.
> (II, ii, 383-84)

Love is idolatry, fascination with an other in whose image I identify myself. Captivation with the love object implies a further dependence on an analogic chain of signifiers, on the very patriarchal order from which one seeks escape. The idol, however, is the projection of one's own gaze and the effect of a purely private voyeurism. It is the image of one's own creation, the self's own image. Hence, where obedience to the patriarchal order implies self-effacement, fantasy becomes the ultimate narcissistic indulgence. Already eroticized, history is subordinated to the foreplay of the imagination:

> Excité d'un désir curieux,
> Cette nuit je l'ai vue arriver en ces lieux,
> Triste, levant au ciel ses yeux mouillés de larmes,
> Qui brillaient au travers des flambeaux et des armes;
> Belle sans ornements, dans le simple appareil
> D'une beauté qu'on vient d'arracher au sommeil.
> Que veux-tu? Je ne sais si cette négligence,
> Les ombres, les flambeaux, les cris et le silence,
> Et le farouche aspect de ses fiers ravisseurs,
> Relevaient de ses yeux les timides douceurs.
>
> (385-94)

Néron's uncertain interpretation of this scene and his feelings of self-doubt create a margin of error for his fantasy to take hold. Extending his gaze towards Junie in the distance, Néron's narrative signals his rite of passage out of the oedipal triangle. Indeed his re-presentation of the scene is his first penetration of history, his first *jouissance*. Néron here enters the history imposed on him by his mother, the feminine order whose cyclical mirrorings exclude him. As Doubrovsky has observed, Néron undertakes a double transfer of power: that of love from mother to lover and that of power from mother to son. Néron attempts to assume his mother's power and return woman to her rightful place in the symbolic:

> Quoi qu'il en soit, ravi d'une si belle vue,
> J'ai voulu lui parler, et ma voix s'est perdue:
> Immobile, saisi d'un long étonnement,
> Je l'ai laissé passer dans son appartement.
> J'ai passé dans le mien. C'est là que, solitaire,
> De son image en vain j'ai voulu me distraire.
> Trop présente à mes yeux je croyais lui parler;

> J'aimais jusqu'à ses pleurs que je faisais couler.
> Quelquefois, mais trop tard, je lui demandais grâce:
> J'employais les soupirs, et même la menace.
> Voilà comme, occupé de mon nouvel amour,
> Mes yeux, sans se fermer, ont attendu le jour.
>
> (395-406)[18]

In this momentary shift from the real to the imaginary that is his representation of the dream, Néron consummates his love with an indifferent victim. The levels of frustration in this text are multiple, for even in his dreams Néron's pleasure depends on his violation of the woman he wishes to captivate. Crossing with his mind's eye the distance that history imposes, he enters the space of Junie's captivity only to be rejected by her. His desire for a captive Agrippine is denied by the very sleeplessness of his night, as this prohibits the extension of the waking dream to the more extensive pleasure of the dream. Captivation and capture are, finally, one and the same.[19]

In all important respects the Oriental play reverses the structures of the Roman one. No counterpart exists for Néron's fantasy. In *Bajazet* the characters act out their desires before us in the full expanse of the stage, maneuvering their pawns and confidants until the entire plot is known by all. Still, the transgressions that occur within the seraglio create the impression of a fiction within the fiction of the play. And the seraglio's enclosed space allows the fiction to be played out for real.

Néron's fantasy reveals a unique repetition compulsion which determines identity, representation, and interpretation. Likewise, in *Bajazet* Amurat's plot to kill Bajazet puts an end to the plotting inside the seraglio. Yet in this play Orcan's counter-espionage effectively disarms the players and destabilizes the mimetic code. Though it assimilates all actions into a uniform progression, this order cannot explain away the difference of the initial act that is itself double:

> Roxane est-elle morte?
>   Oui, j'ai vu l'assassin
> Retirer son poignard tout fumant de son sein.
> Orcan, qui méditait ce cruel stratagème,
> La servait à dessein de la perdre elle-même.
>
> (V, xi, 1675-78)

Bajazet presents a negative repetition: transgression mirrors transgression. Thus while history affects fiction, the opposite is also true. Because we have come to regard the Father as Law, we accept the widescale violence that Amurat sets in motion as necessary for the tragedy's resolution. Let us not forget, however, that this violence was equally the cause of the tragedy. Amurat's decision to have Bajazet murdered transforms government into as self-serving an enterprise as any undertaken by Narcisse or Acomat. Unlike these counselors, Amurat has right on his side since he is the designated authority. The true test of tolerance, however, occurs precisely with those who enjoy power. And here, Barthes is right to insist, the Father inspires a reign of terror:

> Le Sérail est comme le monde: l'homme s'y débat contre l'incertitude des signes, sous le regard d'un Pouvoir qui les change à son caprice. Atalide, Roxane, Bajazet, Acomat sont des aveugles; ils cherchent avec angoisse dans l'autre un signe clair. Et pourtant ces victimes sont des bourreaux: ils tuent sous le regard de qui va les tuer.[20]

The reaffirmation of the Father's control is therefore not sufficient to reduce the explosive effects of the performance itself. The message relayed to Amurat and the incriminating letter found with Atalide convey, respectively, the truth outside the seraglio and the fiction within. The fact of this fiction, though, is false, as the spaces are interdependent. We learn of the deaths of Roxane, Bajazet, and Atalide while watching a stage to which the Father never returns. In this doubled absence we observe the obscuring effects of a Law that provides neither truth nor revelation. Imitation, Zaïde instructs us by her example, is the frustrated search for the other, unrealizable even in death:

> Ah! madame!...Elle expire. O ciel! en ce malheur
> Que ne puis-je avec elle expirer de douleur!
> (V, xii, 1747-48)

The "I" of the Intertext

Derrida has argued that one writes in a language and in a logic whose ordering system speech cannot dominate absolutely.[21] All language, he maintains, and all who speak it are caught in the double bind of history such that revolt can be conceived only in the terms of the order against which it is undertaken:

> Si l'*Ordre* dont nous parlons est si puissant, si sa puissance est unique en son genre, c'est précisément par son caractère sur-déterminant et par l'universelle, la structurale, l'universelle et infinie complicité en laquelle il compromet tous ceux qui l'entendent en son langage, quand même celui-ci leur procure encore la forme de leur dénonciation. L'ordre alors est dénoncé dans l'ordre.[22]

In my readings of *Britannicus* and *Bajazet* I have attempted to show the disorder provoked by the ordering system(s). To argue that revolt in *Bajazet* more effectively influences historical consciousness is to imply a distinction, a difference in representation, which may be called Orientalism. The Oriental represents a reversability because its simplest structure is itself double: both/and. There is a reciprocity of Law and language, a correspondence between the collective symbolic order and the universal order of language. Néron's desire is determined by Law; to enter the symbolic is equivalent to learning the Name-of-the-Father. Yet Roxane shows not only the possibility that desire is determined by the social but also that Law itself functions as a constituent element of desire.

To re-present, as I have attempted here, Derrida's critique of Foucault's reading of Descartes is to establish a discursive cycle that imitates tragedy's own structure.[23] Looking back across Derrida and Foucault to a portion of the *Discours,* we discover a scene of representation that is a model for the doubting subject. This is the truth about representation that the (re)readings of Descartes and Racine with Derrida and Foucault guarantee. The certainty of doubt is what allows Descartes and Racine, like those of us who look for truth about ourselves in their writings, to escape the simple repetition of an inherited idea that is a tragedy unperformed:

> ...je jugeai que, pour tout le reste de mes opinions, je pouvais librement entreprendre de m'en défaire....Et en toutes les neuf années

suivantes, je ne fis autre chose que rouler ça et là dans le monde, tâchant
d'y être spectateur plutôt qu'acteur en toutes les comédies qui s'y
jouent; et faisant particulièrement réflexion, en chaque matière, sur ce
qui la pouvait rendre suspecte, et nous donner occasion de nous
méprendre, je déracinais cependant de mon esprit toutes les erreurs qui
s'y étaient pu glisser auparavant. (pp. 28-29)

If the pleasure of de-racin(e)-ation can be appreciated only in the
present context, Descartes's description has much in common with even the
audience of Racine's own time. Those who went to see his works did not
do so with the intention of doubting anything at all, but the theater imposed
this suspension of belief on them. The prejudice in their case was the
inferiority of the Orient. To some extent, certainly, the Orientals were the
ultimate scapegoats of the classical theater. Their desires substituted for the
audience's own: catharsis was a sparing. It was likewise a purging,
however, and produced the spectator's strong identification with the
characters on stage. Governed by the same mimetic laws, the same
patriarchal tradition, the Orient could not be dismissed as a purely external
corruption.

The conflicting demands of identification and distantiation further
situate Descartes within the theater of his own performance (autobiography)
as within the theater of Racine. Descartes's representation is, at first glance,
the inverted image of Néron's captivation. Descartes willfully adopts the
spectator's role from which Néron seeks escape. Otherwise, the mirrorings
between the two texts reinforce a representation of the same. That is,
Descartes's deliberate decision to distance himself so as to know the truth is
the very situation which Néron experiences as the trap of representation:
desire is displaced along the analogic chain that we now, after Lacan, call
the symbolic. For the scientist this is equally problematic because he is in
the false position of believing himself to be outside a situation that actually
is mediating.

We can better understand Descartes's autobiographical insertions,
therefore, as necessary supplements to the truth that he uncovers. Indeed,
though he argues against imitation, his endeavors to make himself appear
inimitable have the effect of imposing a law of imitation upon the reader:

...bien que j'aie souvent expliqué quelques-unes de mes opinions à des
personnes de très bon esprit, et qui, pendant que je leur parlais,
semblaient les entendre fort distinctement, toutefois, lorsqu'ils les ont

redites, j'ai remarqué qu'ils les ont changées presque toujours en telle
sorte que je ne les pouvais plus avouer pour miennes. (p. 69)

The thinking subject constitutes itself in relation to a hypothetical
other so as to become this other that constitutes the self. Representation
inevitably binds Descartes to the discovery of the already known in the same
way that the symbolic, although an infinite representation, confines the
subject to Law. Judovitz argues that Descartes restricts his evidence to the
"measure of his method" since, as Kant, Heidegger, and Lukács have
maintained, the Cogito indicates that "things will only show themselves
insofar as they obey (the) mathematical or axiomatic aperture that
circumscribes them in advance."[24] Yet the representation of representation
is performative and allows Descartes to establish himself in discourse—
dialectic—as it persuades us of his singular presence.

While representation determines subjectivity, it restricts the subject.
The Cogito (Book IV) gives the "I" of the *Discours* the certainty of being
independent of any narrative act.[25] The narrative, however, continues for
two and one half additional books. It supplements the history of
Descartes's life of which the development of the Cogito is a part. But
where the Cogito seals Descartes in an act of solitude, in an absence which,
for a writer, is the reduction to a certain ignominity, the narrative allows him
to assert himself within the representation. Its didactic purpose notwith-
standing, the act of narrating allows Descartes to constitute, beyond
imitation, the performing self.

Roxane's narrative similarly depends on a distinction between the
constitution of the self in representation and the constitution of the self
through representation. In the first instance subjectivity is restricted by a
concept of representation that is subjection, while in the second the
performing subject knows herself as other. To the *ego sum* of representation Roxane, like Descartes, adds the *ego sum alter* of representing:

> Je sais que des sultans l'usage m'est contraire;
> Je sais qu'ils se sont fait une superbe loi
> De ne point à l'hymen assujettir leur foi <...>
> Et moi, qui n'aspirais qu'à cette seule gloire,
> De ses autres bienfaits j'ai perdu la mémoire.
> Toutefois, que sert-il de me justifier?
> Bajazet, il est vrai, m'a tout fait oublier.
> Malgré tous ses malheurs, plus heureux que son frère,

Il m'a plu, sans peut-être aspirer à me plaire:
Femmes, gardes, visir, pour lui j'ai tout séduit;
En un mot, vous voyez jusqu'où je l'ai conduit.
Grâces à mon amour, je me suis bien servie
Du pouvoir qu'Amurat me donna sur sa vie.
                              (I, iii, 290-314)

Afterword

Thoughts for a Performance

IN THE CRITICAL TRADITION IT IS GENERALLY Pascal who shares a common space with Racine,[1] and I now turn to his *Pensées* in order to complete the cycle of re-readings begun in this book with the Renaissance idea of the circle. Pascal establishes the absolute power of God through an infinite representation whose coherence depends on a sustained inquiry into difference:

> On se croit naturellement bien plus capable d'arriver au centre des choses que d'embrasser leur circomférence. L'étendue visible du monde nous surpasse visiblement; mais comme c'est nous qui surpassons les petites choses, nous nous croyons plus capables de les posséder, et cependant il ne faut pas moins de capacité pour aller jusqu'au néant que jusqu'au tout, il la faut infinie pour l'un et l'autre; et il me semble que qui aurait compris les derniers principes des choses pourrait aussi arriver jusqu'à connnaître l'infini. L'un dépend de l'autre, et l'un conduit à l'autre. Ces extrémités se touchent et se réunissent en Dieu, et en Dieu seulement.[2]

If a system of taxonomy and a new leap of faith separate this statement from the concept of the universe maintained one hundred years earlier, it represents the same plenitudinous order. How tragedy, as an art form, fits into this schema is a complex matter, because a sense of tragedy (*misère*) is one of the very problems that Pascal endeavors to have his readers overcome. Corneille constructs piece by abstract piece, play by play, the symmetrical layers of an expanding microstructure. Racine fixes the Father's image at the center of each play and gives us a hero whose violation is proof of ineluctable divine law. Each, then, represents a universe whose proportions appear to correspond very neatly to the

Pascalian model. So we find ourselves in a quandry, wondering whether tragedy is an act of bad faith.

To ask this question is to assert a correlation between Pascal's thoughts on *divertissement* and *misère* and the concepts of *performance* and *tragedy,* respectively. Such is the very limited scope of these concluding remarks. If we allow that Pascal's reflections on man and religion raise interesting problems for the theater, we can situate him with Corneille and Racine in an essay on representation in order to probe further the impact of literature on the classical episteme. To read in this way is to assume, as throughout this book, that literature does not simply mirror a concept of the world informed through science and philosophy but actively contributes to its formulation. Although this investigation into representation engages Pascal and the tragedians in a work on which they never actually collaborated, it is a fitting last performance by means of which to assess the role of the theater for culture and its anthropology.

Pascal's reflections on the misery of man without God include a description of the vice of self-love. His language recalls the conventions of the theater:

> L'homme n'est donc que déguisement, que mensonge et hypocrisie, et en soi-même et à l'égard des autres. Il ne veut donc pas qu'on lui dise la vérité. Il évite de la dire aux autres; et toutes ses dispositions, si éloignées de la justice et de la raison, ont une racine naturelle dans son cœur. (100-978)

Pointing to man's normal state of corruption as a "voluntary illusion," Pascal creates a referent for the theater that is an absence. Involved in elaborate confusions of identity and transgressions which belie nature, the actors on stage imitate a negative model in the real world. The theater authenticates man's corruption and therefore is itself false.

Indeed, this reproach is typically invoked to censor the theater.[3] History joins religion, politics, and drama in a unique representation of power which balances self-interest and sacrifice. From the mysteries of early Christianity to the modern notion of charisma, organized religion and government depend on a leader's ability to convince his subjects that their own interest is best served by sacrificing to him part of their pleasure/ crops/profits. The priest's mystique depends on the promise of an afterlife, the king's on the promise of participation in an "outerlife," a world at once more expansive and secure than the individual is capable of making for himself. And the theater, with its costumes and ceremonies and concentration of the intensity of life into five acts of a performance, recreates this mystique around the figure of the king on stage. But even a king, Pascal insists, is human:

> Le roi est environné de gens qui ne pensent qu'à divertir le roi, et l'empêcher de penser à lui. Car il est malheureux, tout roi qu'il est, s'il y pense (139-136).

Yet on the stage, as on the throne, the king is also other than human. In a seminal study of the Church and the monarchy, Ernst Kantorowicz explains that the sovereign assumes the powers of the priest. The king was both a man of flesh and blood who enjoyed actual political might and a symbolic body in which this power was represented as an absolute, as an idea of the infinite. Formulating a concept of government after the model elaborated by Catholic theology, the State assumed both an imaginary and a real power.[4] Louis Marin has convincingly demonstrated that although Port-Royal insisted on the absolute separation of Church and State, Christ and King, the desire for power as manifest in the representation of the king actually blurred this distinction.[5] Thus when Pascal's king watches a performance by Corneille's or Racine's king, he does not see himself. Nor is the king on stage what he appears to be.

Pascal would sacrifice the king in a ritual performance that sanctifies the Church, thereby undoing the performance that makes the king a God:

> En un mot, le *moi* a deux qualités: il est injuste en soi, en ce qu'il se fait centre de tout, il est incommode aux autres, en ce qu'il les veut asservir: car chaque *moi* est l'ennemi et voudrait être le tyran de tous les autres. (455-597)

The formulation of the ego is identical to a struggle for absolute domination. The king who abuses his power is a tyrant. Marin, however, argues that this relation is but the other side of an original anthropology:

> ...le motif philosophique du propre et de l'appropriation du sujet à soi par ses qualités (le moi) se lit directement dans le motif sociologique et politique de la puissance de la propriété de la personne individuelle et collective, par ses richesses et ses biens, tout comme, à l'inverse, celui

> de la misère et de l'aliénation de la "figure" du sujet se lit dans le motif
> de la dépossession, de l'égarement et de l'impuissance.[6]

This contrast, in its suggestion of the enemy brothers, is equally apposite
for the theater. In Corneille's early works resolution depends on the
generosity of a king recognized as generous, while his later works are
characterized by the tyrannical acts of a prince whose subjects eliminate
him. On Racine's stage, although the king often acts *in absentia* or by
default, the play's resolution produces a collective recognition of his power.
In Corneille's plays a good prince or the Idea of a good prince survives the
evil. Racine's indulgence of the Father's uncertain control results from the
designation of a substitute victim. The king is spared, protected by a divine
right. The theater redeems itself.

Redemption is a compensation, proof that the experience is not
integral. Marin, employing the term "effet de portrait" as Barthes uses
"effet de réel,"[7] shows that Pascal empties the sign (king) and pushes its
object back so far as to refuse mimetic completeness:

> Qu'est-ce donc qu'un roi? C'est un portrait de roi et cela seul le fait roi
> et, par ailleurs, c'est aussi un homme. A quoi il convient d'ajouter que
> l' "effet de portrait", l'effet de représentation, *fait le roi,* en ce sens que
> tout le monde croit que le roi et l'homme ne font qu'un, ou que le
> portrait du roi est seulement l'image du roi. Personne ne sait qu'à
> l'inverse le roi est seulement son image et que, derrière ou au-delà du
> portrait, il n'y a pas le roi, mais un homme. Personne ne sait ce secret
> et le roi moins que tous les autres, peut-être.[8]

So it can be argued that in the theater the king is but the image of a
man. On Corneille's stage the king, although bodily present, is of less
consequence than is the idea of power that he represents. Psychologically
and ideologically less complicated than the heroes whose lives he orders,
the prince suffers no conflict of values and no choice. By these standards,
Auguste is the most anguished of Corneille's kings. But his generous
forgetting once the conspiracy is over stands among the most arbitrary of
Corneille's endings. Yet, as we have seen, Don Fernand's and Tulle's
interpretations of history are also arbitrary judgments which therefore stand
as challenges to knowledge and truth. In the later plays the monarch's
presence is even less forthright; he is a negative model, the tyrant whose

truth is the other side of representation. By *Suréna* the idea of a beneficent prince who protects his subjects against injustice is mere fantasy.

The Father's questionable presence in Racine's works is a point to which this book has turned time and again. In the end the patriarchs all recoup their losses and enjoy a moment of vengeful recovery. Vengeance is their secret. Here, too, however, the fullness of tragedy is denied by what has been described in terms of a disproportionate representation: the failure to determine identities through a chain of resemblances; the emergence of meaning from within the space of repetition.

Perhaps the more pressing question for the theater is "what is a god?" It is a portrait of a god and that alone makes him god and, moreover, it is also a king. The god of tragedy is an effect of representation. This is not because a god is a force that man cannot see; his presence is felt even in his absence. Rather, fidelity, the secular act of faith, assures his presence as part of an infinite representation, an ongoing ritual. But if faith assures at least the chance of salvation, fidelity—because it sets forth the family of man as a chain of portraits that are so many signs that a god, like a king, father, and son, will be sacrificed to representation—assures us that ritual is a negative model. By virtue of this paradigm God will always be part of ritual's contingence, part of the history of tragedy. This is the truth of discourse: on the one hand, the immanence of the sign, on the other, the impossibility of ascribing it a fixed position. Among the most significant effects of an infinite representation as it is structured by ritual, therefore, is the reformulation of the original perception. The theater denies us a single perspective with the characters, the playwright, and the gods. Our disproportion is having to find the center of a stage whose circumference we measure so easily.

The distance that separates us from the center is the truth of representation. Symmetry (from *summetria*—just proportion; *sun,* with, and *metron,* measure) exists only as a quality of time; it is a linear rather than a spatial measure. Divided into five acts which duplicate the ritual cycle, the tragedy is diachronically uniform. The first and fifth acts establish a historical context against which to measure the critical events of the third. But the action is not prescriptive. The locus of the play is a place of revolt that explodes and, if we allow it, disappears. To retain the center, to supplement the cycle with a massive core, is to acknowledge a final discontinuity. Recognizing the weight of the experience, we must admit an inability to abstract from part to whole, from nothingness to infinity.

It is for this reason that the theater cannot, like the liturgy of the Church, be assimilated to ancient ritual. The spectator/reader of the drama, however vicarious his or her involvement, is physically removed from the celebration on stage. Ritual participants and the actors who imitate them can ignore the evil that they commit through their violence because direct participation allows no distance and constitutes no truth. Seated before the stage, the spectator knows that the action resembles but is not the court, that the actors' transgressions occur as part of an imaginary other scene. This is a critical perspective. The dependence of the theater on the spectator's response to complete the performance is the institutionalization of a new freedom. Completing more than the ordering of a signifying chain, more than the description and delimitation of a world of knowledge, perception is knowledge beyond doubt (the refusal of mysticism except as a vehicle to this other truth), knowledge of more than the rigorous equivalences taught by science. Reception is the need to create and contribute to culture the means of rethinking itself; it guarantees an open perspective within a tradition that is self-critical. It is to inscribe all discourse within the cycle of re-readings that measure, in just proportion, the distance between known, knowing, and unknown.

Notes

Introduction

1. John D. Lyons and Stephen G. Nichols, Jr., eds. *Mimesis: From Mirror to Method, Augustine to Descartes* (Hanover: University Press of New England, 1982), p.1. These authors further explain: "For those who see objectivity as its prime function, mimesis constitutes that aspect of the work of art that represents whatever is thought to possess the most concrete reality prior to the activity that brings the work of art into existence: the gesture of painting, of speaking, or of carving....The other view of mimesis does not emphasize the independent existence of the object represented, but rather focuses on the gesture of the person or subject who undertakes to displace our attention from the world of pre-existent objects to the work itself."

2. Lyons and Nichols, p. 3. The authors are referring to Michel Foucault, *L'Archéologie du savoir* (Paris: Gallimard, 1969) and *Les Mots et les choses: Une Archéologie des sciences humaines* (Paris: Gallimard, 1966).

3. Lyons and Nichols, pp. 3-4.

4. Louis Marin, *Le Portrait du roi* (Paris: Minuit, 1981), pp. 10-11. Marin further reasons: "...si la représentation non seulement reproduit en fait mais encore en droit les conditions qui rendent possibles [sic] sa reproduction, alors on comprend l'intérêt du pouvoir à se l'approprier. Représentation et pouvoir sont de même nature."

5. Marin, p. 10.

6. Marin, p. 10, my translation. Unless otherwise indicated, all translations appearing in this book are my own.

7. My use throughout this book of the concept of Law is consistent with the description offered by Mitchell Greenberg, *Detours of Desire: Readings in the French Baroque* (Columbus: Ohio State University Press, 1984), pp. 5-6: "The 'Father,' as 'Law' within patriarchy, stands as the representative of the primary social taboo that founds society—the interdiction of incest. This metaphor, situated as it is at the crossroads of the individual and the social, is 'represented' in the 'persona'—emperor, monarch, priest—who for his subjects, stands cloaked in the prerogatives of the sacred. He is the dispenser of the Law, the arbiter of pleasure, who controls, while remaining above, the imperatives of life and death. As a living representation that validates the place of the individual in the community, the 'king' serves as the mimetic model that, reproduced in art, architecture, and literature, defined the structuring possibilities and limits of subjectivity in classical society. It would perhaps not be too farfetched to suggest that Classicism...is the ritualization of the Law of the Father as a representational imperative." See also Roland Barthes, *Sur Racine* (Paris: Seuil, 1963), pp. 48-50.

8. Here I adapt to tragedy Lyons's and Nichols's argument, p. 3: "We see in works of art and literature not simply the *concentration* of ideas that constitute a cultural identity, but also the potential (or real) *dispersion,* the evasions implicit in those same concepts."

9. Timothy J. Reiss, *Tragedy and Truth: Studies in the Development of a Renaissance and Neoclassical Discourse* (New Haven: Yale University Press, 1980), p. 17, argues that tragedy serves as a container of a particular knowledge concerning the moral and psychological functioning of society and the individual. Asserting that tragedy "by the order of its own performance" names the tragic as a knowable condition, Reiss posits an act of cognition that is purely objective. Reiss's identification of the forms of knowledge made available through tragedy leads him to conclude that in its search to create a referential truth, tragedy "overcomes all internal questioning." Looking past this objective knowledge to the structuring systems which the text and we, as critics, employ to organize it, this study will indicate how tragedy generates internal questioning.

10. Timothy J. Reiss, *The Discourse of Modernism,* (Ithaca: Cornell University Press, 1982), p. 29. Reiss makes a considerable leap beyond even the writings of Foucault, whose influence he acknowledges, to expand dramatically our understanding of the classical episteme.

11. Reflecting its curious suspension between two parallel yet dissimilar configurations—the Renaissance representation of God as the infinite center of an infinite sphere, and Pascal's representation of man's insufficiency through the contrasting proportions of an infinitely divisible natural sphere—French neoclassical tragedy represents difference in the act and art of repetition. Descartes, who dominates the space between the Renaissance and Pascal, transformed the idea of human knowledge by asking his readers to scrutinize their beliefs through the practice of methodical doubt. It is fitting that the Cartesian legacy now extend beyond even the idea of the episteme developed by Foucault to the concept that Lyons and Nichols, p. 3, label representing: the active participation of the reader/spectator in the definition of the work of art. As doubting subjects we become aware of the indeterminacy of the signifying process in any single drama. We shall note that both Corneille's and Racine's tragedies evidence a progressive weakening of the hierarchical structures which bind the action. Heroes become steadily less effective; successive monarchs execute power less efficiently and with declining force; characters move from sacrifice to transgression.

12. At the risk of oversimplification, one can extract from Girard, *La Violence et le sacré* (Paris: Grasset, 1972) the following schema: In an initial stage a community rent with strife locates a sacrificial victim whose death provides catharsis. The victim—either an animal or a human selected from society's marginal class—allows for the elimination of tension without fear of reprisal. The second stage witnesses a "sacrificial crisis," or breakdown of those differences which order society—man/god, man/man, parent/child. Reciprocal acts of violence threaten to destroy society until the expulsion or death of a surrogate victim (*pharmakos*) whose marginal status again assures a period of stability. In *Des Choses cachées depuis la fondation du monde* (Paris: Grasset, 1978), p. 234, Girard insists that the death of Christ, because he dies "non pas dans un sacrifice mais contre tous les sacrifices, pour qu'il n'y ait plus de sacrifices," leads to a new logic of nonviolence which brings an end to the sacred as it grows out of violence.

13. Julia Kristeva, *Pouvoirs de l'horreur: Essai sur l'abjection* (Paris: Seuil, 1980), p. 82, argues: "On peut émettre l'hypothèse qu'un système symbolique (social) *correspond* à une structuration spécifique du sujet parlant dans l'*ordre symbolique*. Dire 'correspondre' élide la question de la cause et de l'effet: est-ce le social qui est déterminé par le subjectif, ou vice versa? La dimension subjective-symbolique que nous introduisons ne restitue donc pas une quelconque causalité profonde ou originaire du *système symbolique* social. Elle donne seulement les *effets* et surtout les *bénéfices* pour le sujet parlant d'une organisation symbolique précise et explique peut-être quels sont les mobiles désirants pour le maintien d'une symbolique sociale donnée. En outre, pareille position du problème nous semble avoir l'avantage de ne pas faire du 'système symbolique' la réplique laïque de l' 'harmonie préétablie' ou de l' 'ordre divin', mais de l'enraciner, comme une *variante possible,* dans la seule universalité concrète qui définit l'être parlant: le procès de la signifiance."

14. Marin's discussion, p. 97, of Racine's praise of the king provides an interesting parallel: "Ainsi le roi dans l'éloge de Racine: 'La voie de la négotiation est bien courte sous un prince qui, ayant toujours de son côté la puissance et la raison, n'a besoin pour faire exécuter ses volontés que de les déclarer.' Si tel est, dans son sens plein, l'éloge, si tel est l'éloge du roi, en évitant l'éloge dans le récit, l'éloge du roi se constitue dans le récit comme la fantasmatique de sa propre lecture du récit."

15. Beginning with Simone de Beauvoir, *Le Deuxième sexe,* 2 vols. (Paris: Gallimard, 1949), a woman's history represents her need to emerge from male domination. Luce Irigaray, *Speculum de l'autre femme* (Paris: Minuit, 1974) and Hélène Cixous and Cathérine Clément, *La Jeune née* (Paris: Union Générale d'Editions, 1975) analyze the woman's association with death in terms of a decentering power. More recently, Sarah Kofman, *L'Enigme de la femme: La Femme dans les textes de Freud* (Paris: Editions Galilée, 1980) has argued that sexual difference is a "metaphysical illusion." For a detailed analysis of the feminine in modern theory, see Alice A. Jardine, *Gynesis: Configurations of Woman and Modernity* (Ithaca: Cornell University Press, 1985).

16. Sigmund Freud, "Creative Writers and Day-dreaming," in *The Standard Edition of the Complete Psychological Works of Sigmund Freud,*

James Strachey, ed.; James Strachey, Anna Freud, Alix Strachey, and Alan Tyson, trans., vol. IX (London: Hogarth Press, 1953-74), p. 153, describes this cathartic pleasure: "The writer softens the character of his egoistic day-dreams by altering and disguising it, and he bribes us by the purely formal—that is, aesthetic—yield of pleasure which he offers us in the presentation of his phantasies. We give the name of an *incentive bonus*, or *fore-pleasure*, to a yield of pleasure such as this, which is offered to us so as to make possible the release of still greater pleasure arising from deeper psychical sources. In my opinion, all the aesthetic pleasure which a creative writer affords us has the character of a fore-pleasure of this kind, and our actual enjoyment of an imaginative work proceeds from a liberation of tensions in our minds."

Chapter One

1. Albert Cook, *French Tragedy: The Power of Enactment* (Chicago: Swallow Press, 1981), p. 107, observes: "For Corneille...the persons are always fully public as well as private. The contradictions work out in the open of the tight stage, and no one who is willing to meet the demands of heroic virtue, as nearly all are in the tragedies through *Polyeucte*, goes under to the condition of being a fatal third, or lapses in the sorrow of unifying tenderness and firmness. The abstract balances between *amour* and *devoir*, or between *famille* and *patrie*, or between *Dieu* and *empire*, can constantly skeletalize the poetry because they have done so in the full equivalences of the action."

2. Georges Poulet, *Les Métamorphoses du cercle* (Paris: Plon, 1961), p. xii, notes how profoundly Leonardo da Vinci and Giordano Bruno were influenced by Meister Eckhart's doctrine defining God in each moment and in each place as constituting the center of all moments and of all places such that the maximum is realized in the minimum: "*In divinis quodlibet est in quolibet, et maximum in minimo, et sic fructus in flore. Ratio, quia Deus, ut ait sapiens, est sphaera intellectualis infinita, cujas centrum est ubique, cum circumferentia nusquam, et cujas tot sunt circumferentiae, quot puncta...Sic Deus est totus in qualibet creatura, in una, sicut in omnibus.*" I cite the full text from Denifle, *Archiv für*

Litteratur-und-Kirchengeschichte des Mittelalters, v. II, 1886, p. 571, in Poulet, p. xxvii. Dante, *Paradiso,* XXX, 103-05, writes of God: "E si distende in circular figura / In tanto, che la sua circonferenza / Sarebbe al sol troppo larga cintura." Du Bartas, *Œuvres,* ed. U.T. Holmes, vol. II (University of North Carolina Press, 1938), p. 104, describes God as a "cercle parfait / Dont le centre est partout et sur tout son rond trait." Traherne, *Centuries of Mediations,* ed. B. Dobell (London, 1908), p. 136, extends the circular symbolism to man as the center of an infinite universe: "My Soul is an infinite Sphere in a Centre." See Poulet, pp. ix-xxxi.

3. Serge Doubrovsky, *Corneille et la dialectique du héros* (Paris: Gallimard, 1963).

4. Doubrovsky argues, p. 22, "Toute situation est historique; mais, inversement, toute histoire est transhistorique, parce qu'elle se produit sur le fond inchangeable de l'existence."

5. Pierre Corneille, *Œuvres complètes* (Paris: Seuil, coll. Intégrale, 1963). I, vi, 305-06. All references are to this edition.

6. Cook, p. 85.

7. This passage builds on the consistent opposition of *cœur*/*devoir* established in the opening lines of this speech by Chimène: "On le vante, on le loue, et mon cœur y consent! / Mon honneur est muet, mon devoir impuissant!" (1127-28). To the extent, however, that one's admiration of Rodrigue's heart is an appreciation of its magnanimity, one is evaluating the passion of his act, i.e. his duty *as* passion. *Cœur* becomes the most comprehensive indication of conflict. Read in this light, these lines appear to be structured on the double meaning of *cœur* as the seat of both love and anger in the case of Chimène and as the agent that paradoxically deprives through magnanimity in the case of Rodrigue. The ellipsis of *cœur* in Chimène's reference to her opposed selves is similarly revealing. A united *cœur* is denied by the necessity that the passionate self (*cœur* in the restricted sense) be suppressed for the angry self to be heard. Chimène's characterization of Rodrigue's heart as one that both defends and offends, that exists in a state of self-contradiction, thus characterizes her own heart as well—though the surface of her language does not make a

confrontation of these complications available to either character except in the resolving action.

8. See Barbara Woshinsky, "Rhetorical Vision in *Le Cid,* " *French Forum* IV, 2 (May 1979), pp.147-59.

9. Serge Doubrovsky, "Corneille: masculin/féminin: Réflexions sur la structure tragique" in *Actes de Tucson,* Jean-Jacques Demorest and Lise Leibacher-Ouvrard, eds. (Paris: Biblio 17, 1984), pp. 100-01.

10. Freud, "Mourning and Melancholia," in *The Standard Edition of the Complete Psychological Works of Sigmund Freud,* vol. XIV, pp. 243-58.

11. Doubrovsky, *Corneille et la dialectique du héros,* insists, pp.148-49: "...on s'atteint soi-même dans l'autre et le meurtre est, à la limite, suicide. L'originalité d'Horace, c'est d'avoir compris que la plus haute forme de l'héroïsme et le point où il atteint, en quelque sorte, la perfection, c'est le *fratricide conscient* ." I will argue against this notion of perfection.

12. Doubrovsky, *Corneille et la dialectique du héros,* p. 150.

13. See Doubrovsky's application of this Hegelian model, *Corneille et la dialectique du héros,* pp. 92-96.

14. Mitchell Greenberg, *Corneille, Classicism & The Ruses of Symmetry* (Cambridge: Cambridge University Press, 1987), p. 68.

15. I thus disagree with Doubrovsky, *Corneille et la dialectique du héros,* p. 154: "...Horace achèvera par le meurtre de Camille la mise à mort de Curiace. Il s'agit, en réalité, d'un seul mouvement, en deux temps."

16. Paul Bénichou. *Morales du grand siècle.* (Paris: Gallimard, 1948), p. 114.

17. André Stegmann, *L'Héroïsme cornélien,* vol. II (Paris: Colin, 1968), p. 588. Jean Rousset, *Forme et signification: Essais sur les*

structures littéraires de Corneille à Claudel (Paris: Corti, 1961; rpt. 1979), p. 16, concludes similarly that Pauline and Polyeucte "se retrouvent...au cinquième acte, phase culminante de l'ascension, d'où ils s'élancent pour un dernier bond qui va les unir définitivement, au point suprême de liberté et de triomphe, en Dieu." But what Rousset himself terms the "excessive geometry" of his analysis provides a framework too rigid to appreciate the resonances of the play's final act.

18. Stegmann refers throughout his discussion to Octave Nadal, *Le Sentiment de l'amour dans l'œuvre de Pierre Corneille* (Paris: Gallimard, 1948) and Doubrovsky, *Corneille et la dialectique du héros*.

19. Cf. Doubrovsky, *Corneille et la dialectique du héros*, p. 251: "En mourant pour son Dieu, Polyeucte meurt donc exclusivement pour lui-même."

20. Doubrovsky, *Corneille et la dialectique du héros*, pp. 259-61.

21. Poulet, p. 15.

22. Foucault, *Les Mots et les choses*, p. 40.

23. David F. Hult, ed. *Concepts of Closure, Yale French Studies* 67 (1984), p. iv.

24. Greenberg, p. 70.

25. Greenberg, p. 87.

Chapter Two

1. Kristeva, p. 20.

2. Corneille is more ambivalent than even Bénichou would allow, p. 42: "...Cléopâtre, folle selon le sens commun, ne l'est pas moins si on la juge selon la mesure des héros: elle a lancé au monde un défi dont elle ne

peut guère se tirer à son honneur. Qui prétend agir contre l'ordre des choses ne peut vaincre que par exception; semblable victoire, si par hasard elle se produit, ne saurait avoir une valeur d'exemple; et ce qui n'est pas exemplaire ne vaut rien en morale." Cf. Stegmann, p. 424: "Cléopâtre est coupable dans ses actes. Mais la *source* de ses actions détestables est 'grandeur d'âme,' puisqu'elle a le courage de cette rupture avec les sentiments naturels intéressés...."

3. Doubrovsky, *Corneille et la dialectique du héros,* p. 296, argues that vengeance undermines the monarchy: "...la passion 'politique', à laquelle tout sentiment naturel est censé être sacrifié, est, chez Cléopâtre, suspecte. Le projet monarchique, en effet, est une fin à lui-même, qui doit se garder pure de toute contamination par une émotion étrangère."

4. Doubrovsky, *Corneille et la dialectique du héros,* p. 298, is less severe in his judgment of Rodogune, who, he argues, is the "seul personnage qui...soit...digne de régner, parce que pas un instant elle ne permet au projet monarchique de se contaminer au contact du sentiment." Doubrovsky would de-emphasize her "déchéance" in favor of her dedication to an ideal. It should be noted, however, that Rodogune remains intent on her demands through the time elapsed between Acts III and IV, at which point she yields to the pressures of love. Responding to Antiochus provides her emotional satisfaction, and thus moves her further from the model of sacrifice and heroic virtue.

5. Two plays from this period which I do not discuss—*Don Sanche* and *Pertharite*—similarly link the problem of identity to political imperatives. Resolution in *Don Sanche*, moreover, offers another example of incest avoided. For a discussion of the interaction between the erotic and the political in the plays of Corneille's middle period, see John D. Lyons's chapter on *Héraclius* in his *A Theatre of Disguise: Studies in French Baroque Drama (1630-1660)* (Columbia, South Carolina: French Literature Publications Company [Summa Publications], 1978), pp. 107-37.

6. Girard, *Des Choses cachées depuis la fondation du monde*, p. 74, insists: "Les règles de ce que nous appelons l' 'intronisation royale' sont celles du sacrifice; elles visent à faire du roi une victime apte à canaliser l'antagonisme mimétique...."

7. This cyclical effect is further sustained by what Corneille would have a weakness in his design: "mais je n'ai pas pu avoir assez d'adresse pour faire entendre les équivoques ingénieux dont est rempli tout ce que dit Héraclius à la fin du premier acte" (*Héraclius,* Examen). Corneille refers to the following lines, whose double meaning can be appreciated only upon rereading the text: "Je te connais, Léonce, et mieux que tu ne crois: / Je sais ce que tu vaux, et ce que je te dois. / Son bonheur est le mien, Madame; et je vous donne / Léonce et Martian en la même personne: / C'est Martian en lui que vous favorisez" (I, iv, 355-59).

8. Stegmann, p. 385.

9. Lyons argues, p. 114: "The characters' experience and emotion offer no resolution of the problem of the play. Only the artificial—in the fullest dramatic sense of artifice—can impose the hierarchy which the characters so desperately seek."

10. Doubrovsky, *Corneille et la dialectique du héros,* p. 339, insists that in order to preserve the monarchy intact "...Corneille introduira dans la légende une distinction radicalement étrangère à l'universalisme religieux: il dédoublera, en quelque sorte, le personnage d'Œdipe, en lui adjoignant celui de Dircé. Séparant le *faux* monarque du *vrai,* la colère des Dieux frappera l'*usurpateur,* non le roi."

11. Jacques Scherer, *Le Théâtre de Corneille* (Paris: Nizet, 1984), p. 110, underestimates the drama's psychological underpinnings: "(Si Corneille) a développé, plus que ses modèles, tout ce qui concerne la recherche du meurtrier de Laïus, il a par contre cherché à atténuer, dans toute la mesure du possible, les conséquences de l'inceste." The two are inextricably linked.

12. *Œdipe,* Examen.

13. Tobin Siebers, *The Mirror of Medusa* (Berkeley: University of California Press, 1983), p. 108.

14. Girard, *La Violence et le sacré,* p. 279, contends that the argument for an undistinguished victim is the "but manqué" of Freud's

research on the oedipal complex. I compare Corneille's, Freud's, and Girard's readings of Sophocles's *Oedipus Rex* in "Heroic Imperatives and Psychic Mechanisms in *Rodogune, Héraclius,* and *Œdipe,* " *Essays in Literature* 10 (Fall 1983), pp. 283-98.

15. This term is borrowed from Henri-Jacques Stiker, "Le Mode de penser de R. Girard," *Esprit* (avril 1979), p. 54, who uses it in another context.

16. In his reading of Freud, Siebers, p. 140, similarly locates "the subtle evolution of the profane" in a shift from persona to person.

17. Jean-Marie Apostolidès, *Le Prince sacrifié: Théâtre et politique au temps de Louis XIV* (Paris: Minuit, 1985), p. 32.

18. For an elaboration of this argument see Bénichou, pp. 15-119.

19. Girard, *La Violence et le sacré,* p. 192.

20. Apostolidès, p. 89, locates new evidence of the sacred in the monstrous circumstances of Suréna's death: "En acceptant le sacrifice de sa vie, Suréna déclenche l'escalade de la violence; il devient en outre le seul individu sacré et son sacrifice exemplaire déchaînera la violence contenue des autres victimes...." This argument contradicts the movement that I have traced here. Politics prevents the ignorance or suspension of belief on which the sacred depends. Paradoxically, Apostolidès appears to describe the "déchaînement" which for Girard signals the collapse of ritual order, yet neither critic finds evidence of this collapse in the theater.

Chapter Three

1. Charles Mauron, *L'Inconscient dans l'œuvre et la vie de Racine* (Paris: Corti, 1969), p. 52.

2. Prepared to abduct Hermione, Oreste cites as higher authority than the Greek princes the destiny which brings him to Hermione at the time

of her rejection by Pyrrhus. Hermione corrupts her father's authority by using the promise that he extracted from Pyrrhus alternately to assert her claim to him and to disavow her interest in favor of Oreste, whom she engages in a cruel act of vengeance. Pyrrhus, denying that a leader's power lies in his subservience to law, cites the law as proof of his claim to Andromaque. It is his right to dispose of his captive as he wishes.

3. Building on Lévi-Strauss' analysis of myth, Barthes, p. 67, observes: "...le mythe part de contradictions et tend progressivement à leur médiation: la tragédie, au contraire, immobilise les contradictions, refuse la médiation, tient le conflit ouvert...."

4. Cf. Mauron, pp. 62-63: "...dans la mesure où Andromaque résiste, elle se range, avec Hector et Hermione, dans le parti de la fidelité, qui oppose à la vie sa double solution de mort: tantôt le renoncement qui mène au suicide, tantôt la vengeance qui mène au crime. Hector conseille la première, Hermione commande la seconde. Du point de vue psychologique, les deux solutions s'équivalent: c'est toujours la résistance qui frappe et l'amour (objet ou pulsion) qui meurt."

5. Jean Racine, *Œuvres complètes* (Paris: Seuil, coll. Intégrale, 1962). I, iv, 312. All references are to this edition. Barthes, p. 84, underscores the political implications of Pyrrhus's position: "Le poids d'un amour non partagé se confond pour lui avec l'emprise de l'ordre ancien; renvoyer Hermione, c'est expressément passer d'une contrainte collective à un ordre individuel où tout est possible; épouser Andromaque, c'est commencer une *vita nuova* où toutes les valeurs du passé sont en bloc allégrement refusées: patrie, serments, alliances, haines ancestrales, héroïsme de jeunesse, tout est sacrifié à l'exercice d'une liberté, l'homme refuse ce qui s'est fait sans lui...." The same will be shown to be true for Andromaque.

6. "Andromaque trompa l'ingénieux Ulysse, / Tandis qu'un autre enfant, arraché de ses bras, / Sous le nom de son fils fut conduit au trépas" (I, i, 74-76).

7. "Madame, dites-moi seulement que j'espère, / Je vous rends votre fils, et je lui sers de père; / Je l'instruirai moi-même à venger les Troyens" (I, iv, 325-27).

8. Cf. "Et qui sait ce qu'un jour ce fils peut entreprendre? (I, ii, 161); "Un enfant malheureux, qui ne sait pas encor / Que Pyrrhus est son maître, et qu'il est fils d'Hector!" (I, iv, 271-72).

9. For an excellent discussion of fidelity and interpretation see Richard Goodkin, "A Choice of Andromache's " in *Concepts of Closure,* pp. 225-47.

10. Cf. "Il m'aurait tenu lieu d'un père et d'un époux" (I, iv, 279).

11. I thus disagree with Barthes, p. 81, that "c'est parce qu'Andromaque n'est pas une mère, mais une amante, que la tragédie est possible."

12. Leo Spitzer, *Etudes de style,* E. Kaufholtz, A. Coulon, M. Foucault, trans. (Paris: Gallimard, 1980), p. 209, observes: "...la langue racinienne est une langue à sourdine. Le premier parmi ces effets de sourdine dans le style de Racine est la DESINDIVIDUALISATION PAR L'ARTICLE INDEFINI (ou au pluriel par *des*)." He indicates, p. 210, the rhetorical power of the text cited: "...les sentiments réprimés s'emparent de l'expression linguistique et renforcent la dynamique de ces articles UN et DES, en eux-mêmes généraux et dénués de passion: derrière cette modestie et cette réserve, on entend l'appel à la justice et au droit, la déclamation rhétorique. Le refoulement des sentiments accentue par réaction le dynamisme de l'expression que le mot exerce sur les sentiments."

13. Lucien Goldmann, *Situation de la critique racinienne* (Paris: l'Arche, 1971), p. 61, makes this same point.

14. Mauron, p. 59, contends further that her sustained antagonism towards Pyrrhus is the probable explanation for Racine's revision of the final scene that showed Andromaque's tears for Pyrrhus. In the earlier version Andromaque cries in outrage to Hermione: "Vous avez trouvé seule une sanglante voie / De suspendre en mon cœur le souvenir de Troie. / Plus barbare aujourd'hui qu'Achille et que son fils. / Vous me faites pleurer mes

plus grands ennemis." It is in light of what Mauron argues is Andromaque's "rigoureuse unité" that Barthes's analysis of the play's resolution appears unconvincing. Though he explains that he need not refer to the earlier version of the scene, Barthes, p. 86, does cite it in support of the statement that he sees Racine making "sans équivoque" in the extant versioi.. "Andromaque prend expressément le relève de Pyrrhus. Pyrrhus mort, elle décide de vivre et de régner, non comme amante enfin débarrassée d'un tyran odieux, mais comme veuve véritable, comme héritière légitime du trône de Pyrrhus. La mort de Pyrrhus n'a pas libéré Andromaque, elle l'a initiée: Andromaque a fait sa conversion, elle est libre." I submit that her freedom is qualified by the fact that the authority she would exercise links Pyrrhus's death to Hector's; i. e., it returns her to the source of her pain. Andromaque is still entrapped within a traditional distribution of roles, still a nurturer, or supporter, of the cycle whose only real freedom appears to be to repeat itself.

15. Cook, p. 52, details these failed correspondences as follows: "...Pyrrhus, who thought he would be marrying either Andromaque or Hermione, is killed at the hands of (Oreste's accomplices). Oreste, who thought he would be rewarded by a Hermione who might or might not love him for murdering her unfaithful lover, finds himself abandoned by her and pursued anew by the Furies, who are identified with his beloved. Hermione, who thought herself to have either Pyrrhus or revenge, finds an impulsive suicide after confronting the bloody corpse. And Andromaque, who expected either death for her son and herself or else a complicated death to save his life, finds herself once more the widow performing...the necessary duties for her dead husband."

16. "Dois-je oublier Hector privé de funérailles, / Et traîné sans honneur autour de nos murailles?" (III, viii, 993-94).

17. "C'est Hector, disait-elle en l'embrassant toujours; / Voilà ses yeux, sa bouche, et déjà son audace; / C'est lui-même, c'est toi, cher époux, que j'embrasse" (II, v, 652-54).

18. Reinhard Kuhn, "The Palace of Broken Words: Reflections of Racine's *Andromaque*," *Romanic Review* LXX, 4 (Nov. 1979), p. 342, refers to "the interplay of surrogates in which everyone acts by proxy." He

links these substitutions to the characters' deceptive language and broken promises.

19. Girard, *La Violence et le sacré,* p. 147. Kuhn, p. 336, reinforces the notion of predicted violence by insisting that "the reader knows...the child will be torn from the mother's protective bosom in order to be flung to death from the walls of Troy. It must be another child, Ascanius, who will assure the reincarnation of Ilion, while the remains of Astyanax will remain buried forever under the incinerated rubble of Troy, despite the efforts of Seneca, Ronsard, and Leo Bersani to disinter them."

20. "Lui, votre père! Après son horrible dessein, / Je ne le connais plus que pour votre assassin" (III, vi, 999-1000); "Dois-je au superbe Achille accorder la victoire? / Son téméraire orgueil que je vais redoubler, / Croira que je lui cède et qu'il m'a fait trembler..." (IV, viii, 1454-56).

21. Girard, *Des Choses cachées depuis la fondation du monde,* p. 140.

22. Jacques Scherer, *Racine et/ou la cérémonie.* (Paris: P. U. F., 1982), p. 25.

23. Scherer, p. 11, cites the first *Dictionnaire* of the Académie française (1694) which defines ceremony not only as a spectacle but as "la transmission d'un pouvoir, ou du moins d'un sentiment doté d'une efficacité véritable."

24. "C'est moi, prince, c'est moi dont l'utile secours / Vous eût du labyrinthe enseigné les détours" (II, v, 655-56); "J'aime, j'aime, il est vrai, malgré votre défense. / Aricie à ses lois tient mes vœux asservis" (IV, ii, 1122-23).

25. Mauron, pp. 153-54. For a more detailed study of the identity of Phèdre and Aricie, see Charles Mauron, *Phèdre* (Paris: Corti, 1968), pp. 63-65.

26. "Madame, pardonnez. J'avoue en rougissant / Que j'accusais à tort un discours innocent" (II, v, 667-68).

27. "Je devrais faire ici parler la vérité, / Seigneur; mais je supprime un secret qui vous touche. / Approuvez le respect qui me ferme la bouche" (IV, ii, 1088-90).

28. Girard, *La Violence et le sacré,* p. 149.

29. Barthes, p. 116.

30. Kristeva, p. 6.

31. Kristeva, p. 149.

32. Kristeva, p. 148ff.

33. Kristeva, pp. 153-54, explains that confession is responsible for turning sin into art; it gives the sinnners "la chance de vivre, ouvertement et intérieurement à l'écart, la joie de leur débordement mis en signe...."

Chapter Four

1. As used here, imitation suggests an organizing principle far more complex than is implied by either Plato's distinction between mimesis and diegesis or by modern realism. Plato contrasts mimetic narrative in which the characters speak, directly, as in drama, with diegetic, or pure narrative in which the poet speaks in his own name without giving the impression that someone else is talking. Racine's narratives are "impure" to the extent that the diegesis typically contains fragments of dialogue. Even in the modern sense, Racine presents a "mimetic diegesis," or mixed narrative that combines events narrated and the instance of narration. Mirroring a society in which the son must model himself after his father, Racine's diegesis is thrice mimetic: recurring patterns represent a history whose present must re-present the past. See Gérard Genette, *Figures III* (Paris: Seuil, 1972). Nina C. Ekstein, *Dramatic Narrative: Racine's Récits* (New York: Peter Lang, 1986) applies narrative theory specifically to the Racine corpus.

2. Nancy K. Miller, "Emphasis Added: Plots and Plausibilities in Women's Fiction," *PMLA* 96 (Jan. 1981), p. 36.

3. Julia Kristeva, *Recherches pour une sémanalyse* (Paris: Seuil, 1969), pp. 208-16.

4. Gérard Genette, *Figures II* (Paris: Seuil, 1969), pp. 74-75. Cited in Miller.

5. Miller observes, p. 36, "...the critical reaction to any given text is hermeneutically bound to another preexistent text: the *doxa* of socialities. Plausibility then is an effect of reading through a grid of concordance."

6. Mauron, *Phèdre*, pp.161-62, details an elaborate list of parallels that structure these plays. Phèdre and Athalie "apparaissent sur scène dans le même état de trouble, de faiblesse physique, d'abattement, d'irrésolution. L'une confie son mal à Œnone, l'autre à Mathan (deux personnages de mauvais conseillers, de doubles sombres). Dans les deux cas le mal est une vision obsédante; son irruption a bouleversé l'esprit de la reine; dans les deux cas, elle est liée à l'image d'un temple, car un Dieu l'a voulue, et l'intuition qu'en a la victime la pousse vers l'autel où vainement, pour éviter le sort fatal, elle présente ses offrandes. La vision est celle d'un adolescent, puis d'un enfant, à la fois charmant et redoutable, auquel on offre une tendresse maternelle, et qui ne répond à cet intérêt que par l'horreur, la haine, la condamnation, le meurtre justicier. Egalement fascinées, les deux reines hésitent entre la fuite et la persécution, puis tentent de séduire ce 'superbe ennemi', connaissent 'd'un refus l'insupportable injure', offrent enfin, en compromis, le partage du pouvoir. Mais chaque avance refusée les engage un peu plus vers le conflit, la persécution réciproque. C'est alors que le père et son Dieu interviennent, sauvant le fils dans *Athalie*, et le faisant périr dans *Phèdre*." I shall contend that these parallels account only for the surface design of the plays. A focus on seduction reveals Phèdre and Athalie to enjoy in fact very different relations with the son and very similar relations to God the Father.

7. Sigmund Freud, "Screen Memories," in *The Standard Edition of the Complete Psychological Works of Sigmund Freud,* vol. III, p. 320, defines a screen memory as "one which owes its value as a memory not to

its own content but to the relation existing between that content and some other, that has been suppressed." My analysis will attempt to expose the suppressed content of the memory.

8. Foucault, *Les Mots et les choses*, pp. 32-91.

9. Foucault, *Les Mots et les choses*, pp. 72-74.

10. J. L. Austin, *How to Do Things With Words,* J. O. Ormso and Marina Sbisà, eds. (Cambridge: Harvard University Press, 1975), distinguishes between constative speech acts as facts or states of being that can be proved either true or false, and performative speech acts that accomplish actions through the very process of speaking. Austin nevertheless concludes that all constative speech is performative since it informs or affirms information.

11. Francesco Orlando, *Toward a Freudian Theory of Literature: With an Analysis of Racine's "Phèdre."* Charmaine Lee, trans. (Baltimore: Johns Hopkins University Press, 1978), p. 71.

12. Cook, p. 38.

13. Shoshana Felman, *Le Scandale du corps parlant: Don Juan avec Austin ou La Séduction en deux langues* (Paris: Seuil, 1980), p. 108.

14. Mauron, *L'Inconscient dans l'œuvre et la vie de Racine,* p. 154, argues that Phèdre and Hippolyte are joined in a reciprocally incestuous relation.

15. Jacques Lacan, *Ecrits* (Paris: Seuil, 1966), pp. 555-57.

16. *Logique de Port-Royal,* Part I, chapter IV. Cited in Foucault, *Les Mots et les choses,* p. 78. In an insightful study of the *Logique,* Louis Marin, *La Critique du discours* (Paris: Minuit, 1975) discovers that even this model of representation is not grounded in a rational strategy.

17. Joad's allusion to Abraham's sacrifice of Isaac (IV, v) incorporates the future murder of Zacharie into the drama.

18. Eléonore M. Zimmermann, "Au delà d'*Athalie*," *French Forum* V, 1 (Jan. 1980), pp. 14-21, offers a perceptive reading of disillusionment and fatality in this play.

19. One might argue that Zacharie substitutes for a repressed wish to be the object of the mother's desire. Yet this, too, signals a breakdown in the symbolic order. Athalie, I argue below, is a mother who refuses to accommodate the son's entry into the symbolic.

20. Mauron, *L'Inconscient dans l'œuvre et la vie de Racine,* p. 298, concludes, "...la beauté d'Athalie, sa réalité, sa palpitation humaine lui vient de ce qui demeure, malgré tout, en elle de féminin et de maternel—bref, de ce qu'elle garde, encore, de Phèdre."

21. Irigaray, p. 165.

22. Irigaray, pp. 26-27.

Chapter Five

1. Barthes, p. 99.

2. Writing specifically about the relationship between France and China in the seventeenth century, Basil Guy, *The French Image of China Before and After Voltaire* (Geneva: Droz, 1963), p. 11, contends that the expansion of commercial interests and the prominent role of the Christian missionaries in China resulted in France's one-sided view of the Orient: "Whether that example [sic] were composed of French ideas on Chinese religion, morality, and politics or on Chinese art, it matters little, since the mistaken—if not wilfully false—interpretation of the Oriental Empire by the inheritors of the Renaissance was almost universally accepted, from the time of the first voyages of discovery to the French Revolution." More recently, in a controversial study of Europe's relation to the East during the nineteenth and twentieth centuries, Edward W. Said, *Orientalism* (New York: Vintage Books, 1979), p. 40, argues that Europe represented the Oriental as living "in a different but thoroughly organized world of his own,

a world with its own national, cultural, and epistemological boundaries and principles of internal coherence. Yet what gave the Oriental's world its intelligibility and identity was not the result of his own efforts but rather the whole complex series of knowledgeable manipulations by which the Orient was identified by the West."

3. Pierre Martino, *L'Orient dans la littérature française au XVIIè et au XVIIIè siècle* (Paris: Librairie Hachette, 1906), p. 15. See also Marie Louise Dufrenoy, *L'Orient romanesque en France,* 2 vols. (Montréal: Beauchemin, 1946-47).

4. Foucault, *Les Mots et les choses,* p. 92.

5. Marin, *Le Portrait du roi,* p. 10.

6. René Descartes, *Discours de la méthode* in *Œuvres de Descartes,* vol. VI, Charles Adam et Paul Tannery, eds. (Paris: Vrin, 1957-68), p. 10. All references to Descartes are to this edition. I have modernized the French spelling.

7. John D. Lyons, "Subjectivity and Imitation in the *Discours de la méthode,*" *Neophilologus* 66 (1982), pp. 508-24. For a discussion of the autobiographical subject in the *Discours,* see also Jean-Luc Nancy, *Ego sum* (Paris: Aubier Flammarion, 1979) and Dalia Judovitz, *Subjectivity and Representation: The Origins of Modern Thought in Descartes* (Cambridge: Cambridge University Press, 1987).

8. Dalia Judovitz, "Autobiographical Discourse and Critical Praxis in Descartes," *Philosophy and Literature* 5 (Spring 1981), p. 93. Judovitz cites Martin Heidegger, *Nietzsche,* vol. 2 (Pfullingen: Neske, 1961): "In fact the enunciated terms (*enoncé*) *cogito me cogitare* leads to mis-understanding, that is to say that he who/represents/himself finds himself represented in all representation *with* his act of representing, justly expressing the *essential* appurtenance of the one who represents himself, to the constitution of representation."

9. Lyons, "Subjectivity and Imitation in the *Discours de la méthode,*" p. 522, explains: "The danger of reading, earlier mentioned by

Descartes, was that the reader might lose himself in the text, might identify too completely with a figure that would estrange him from himself and finish like the *extravagant* hero of a romance. Here, in Part VI, the author expresses the opposite fear—that the reader may modify the text according to his own understanding. The reader who transforms opinions to suit himself has avoided the danger of surrender to a text, but now the author fears a loss. The reader's opinions are no longer those of the author."

10. Serge Doubrovsky, "L'Arrivée de Junie dans *Britannicus:* La Tragédie d'une scène à l'autre, " *Littérature* 32 (déc. 1978), p. 28.

11. Kristeva, *Pouvoirs de l'horreur: Essai sur l'abjection,* p. 43.

12. Barthes, observing that the space of the tragedy is necessarily closed, insists, p. 104: "En un mot, le Sérail, par sa double fonction de prison et de contiguïté, exprime sans cesse ce mouvement contradictoire d'abandon et de reprise, d'exaspération et de frustration qui définit le tourment racinien: c'est là le côté 'oriental' de Racine: le Sérail est littéralement la caresse étouffante, l'étreinte qui fait mourir."

13. Sir Paul Rycaut, *Histoire de l'empire ottoman* (Amsterdam: David Mortier, 1714); cited in Martino, p. 137.

14. Cf. Martino pp. 208-09: "...il n'y a pour (Bajazet) une seule résolution possible, ce serait de proposer un partage; il aimera Atalide et donnera de l'amour à Roxane! et peut-être voudrait-il en répétant sans cesse ses 'hélas!' et ses 'que faire?' insinuer à ses amantes une solution qu'il se sent capable d'accepter. A ce point de vue, le personnage n'aurait guère de moralité...européenne; et le public aurait difficilemeent supporté que Racine insistât trop sur des indications de ce genre. Elles y sont néanmoins et, par elles, le caractère de Bajazet reçoit une vérité, ou, si l'on veut, une vraisemblance qu'on lui a quelquefois refusée."

15. Mauron, *L'Inconscient dans l'œuvre et la vie de Racine,* p. 95, reminds us that Segrais's "Floridon, ou l'Amour imprudent," published in 1657 and a probable source for Racine, likewise depends on the characters' agreement to share their love. Indeed, without this contract, Segrais's scenario would resemble *Phèdre:* "D'abord, Roxane y est une sultane mère.

Elle règne en l'absence du sultan Amurat et s'éprend du très jeune Bajazet.... Celui-ci devient son amant sur les conseils de l'eunuque Acomat. Cependant, Bajazet aime Floridon, esclave favorite de la sultane. Roxane, ainsi trahie, consent d'abord à un partage, protège même son amant contre un premier messager de mort envoyé par Amurat." Even when Bajazet fails to respect the terms of their agreement, vengeance for Roxane takes the form of another sharing. "Floridon survit; elle élève même son fils avec l'aide de la sultane, qui règne encore longtemps après la disparition d'Amurat." Martino's denial, p. 199, that Racine was inspired by Segrais appears highly unlikely in light of these parallels.

16. See Orlando's extensive analysis of negation.

17. Doubrovsky, "L'Arrivée de Junie dans *Britannicus,*" p. 29, distinguishes the following series of narrative re-presentations: the "parole du désir, en tant que désir de parole" as Néron's speech to Narcisse substitutes for it, "ouvre l'espace de la *représentation qui se joue sur la scène,* elle-même articulée à l'absence de *deux autres scènes:* <1> La scène réelle (vue de Junie) <2> la scène imaginaire (scène nocturne de Néron). La scène verbale <3>, qui est celle du récit auquel nous assistons, s'articule aux deux premières en ce qu'elle y résout effectivement l'impossibilité de parler qui traverse les deux autres ('J'ai voulu lui parler'; 'je croyais lui parler')."

18. Doubrovsky, "L'Arrivée de Junie dans *Britannicus,*" p. 35, explains: "Quand Néron dit qu'il se fait 'une très belle image', c'est qu'en effet, l'image est *trop belle* pour convenir à son objet, lequel n'est certes pas cette belle fille dévêtue, sur qui le regard ne fait que se poser; elle paraît 'avec trop d'avantage', pour la simple raison qu'à travers Junie, qu'il voit ou imagine, c'est *Agrippine* qui est inconsciemment visée et investie, terme ultime du désir de Néron...Les repères identificatoires sont ici flagrants. *Tous les rapports que Néron (re)joue avec Junie sont exactement ceux qui ont toujours déjà joués entre lui et sa mère.* "

19. Narcisse (the narcissus) reinforces the self's alienation in the imaginary: "Mais je m'en fais peut-être une trop belle image: / Elle m'est apparue avec trop d'avantage: / Narcisse, qu'en dis-tu? Quoi, seigneur! croira-t-on / Qu'elle ait pu si longtemps se cacher à Néron?" (407-10).

20. Barthes, p. 101.

21. Jacques Derrida, *De la grammatologie* (Paris: Minuit, 1967), p. 227.

22. Jacques Derrida, *L'Ecriture et la différence* (Paris: Seuil, 1967), p. 58. Derrida refers to Michel Foucault, *Histoire de la folie à l'âge classique.*

23. Derrida, *De la grammatologie*, p. 226, argues that there are no simple origins: "A travers cette séquence de suppléments s'annonce une nécessité: celle d'un enchaînement infini, multipliant inéluctablement les médiations supplémentaires qui produisent le sens de cela même qu'elles diffèrent: le mirage de la chose même, de la présence immédiate, de la perception originaire. L'immédiateté est dérivée. Tout commence par l'intermédiaire, voilà ce qui est 'inconcevable à la raison.' " Although we perceive the performance directly, the reading of signs which is our perception testifies to the supplemental activity outlined by Derrida.

24. Judovitz, "Autobiographical Discourse and Critical Praxis in Descartes," p. 103. Judovitz concludes, however, that the concept of representation is restricted to the absolute subjectivity of a universal figure.

25. Lyons, "Subjectivity and Imitation in the *Discours de la méthode*," p. 521.

Afterword

1. Lucien Goldmann, *Le Dieu caché: Etude sur la vision tragique dans les "Pensées" de Pascal et dans le théâtre de Racine* (Paris: Gallimard, 1959) offers an exhaustive study.

2. Blaise Pascal, *Pensées*, ed. Brunschvicg (Paris: Garnier Frères, 1964), fragment 72; ed. Lafuma (Paris: Intégrale, 1963), fragment 199. Hereafter, only the fragment numbers of each edition will be given.

3. Apostolidès, p. 52, reminds us that Nicole, Bossuet, and the Prince de Conti objected to the freedom of the theater: "Pour eux, la cérémonie théâtrale est sacrilège; elle parodie la *sacra menta*, le sacrement, puisque les images ne sont pas détachées des choses, comme la théorie de la transubstanciation vient de le confirmer contre les analyses protestantes de l'eucharistie."

4. Ernst H. Kantorowicz, *The King's Two Bodies: A Study in Mediaeval Theology* (Princeton: Princeton University Press, 1957). See also Henri de Lubac, *Corpus mysticum: L'Eucharistie et l'église au moyen age* (Paris: Aubier, 1949). For the relation of these ideas to Pascal's *Pensées,* see Marin, *Le Portrait du roi.* For their connection to the classical theater, see Apostolidès op. cit. and *Le Roi-machine: Spectacle et politique au temps de Louis XIV* (Paris: Minuit, 1981).

5. Marin, *La Critique du discours.*

6. Marin, *Le Portrait du roi*, p. 265.

7. Roland Barthes, "L'Effet de réel," *Communications* 11 (1968), p. 89.

8. Marin, *Le Portrait du roi,* p. 267. Marin extends his analysis in *La Critique du discours,* p. 120: "...l'homme, la vérité, la morale ne sont pas réductibles au modèle de la représentation. En fin de compte, la valeur du modèle sera négative: il indiquera, dans l'homme, la vérité comme l'autre de la représentation."

Bibliography

Apostolidès, Jean-Marie. *Le Prince sacrifié: Théâtre et politique au temps de Louis XIV*. Paris: Minuit, 1985.

——————. *Le Roi-machine: Spectacle et politique au temps de Louis XIV*. Paris: Minuit, 1981.

Arnauld, Antoine et Nicole, Pierre. *La Logique ou l'art de penser contenant outre les règles communes plusieurs observations nouvelles propres à former le jugement*. Paris: Desprez, 1683; rpt. Louis Marin, ed. Paris: Flammarion, 1970.

Austin, J. L. *How to Do Things With Words*. J. O. Ormso and Mrina Sbisà, eds. Cambridge: Harvard University Press, 1975.

Barthes, Roland. "L'Effet de réel." Communications 11 (1968), pp. 84-89.

——————. *Sur Racine*. Paris: Seuil, 1963.

Beauvoir, Simone de. *Le Deuxième sexe*. 2 vols. Paris: Gallimard, 1949.

Bénichou, Paul. *Morales du grand siècle*. Paris: Gallimard, 1948.

Clément, Cathérine et Cixous, Hélène. *La Jeune née*. Paris: Union Générale d'Editions, 1975.

Cook, Albert. *French Tragedy: The Power of Enactment*. Chicago: Swallow Press, 1981.

Corneille, Pierre. *Œuvres complètes*. Paris: Seuil, coll. Intégrale, 1963.

Derrida, Jacques. *De la grammatologie*. Paris: Minuit, 1967.

——————. *L'Ecriture et la différence*. Paris: Seuil, 1967.

Descartes, René. *Œuvres de Descartes*. 13 vols. Charles Adam et Paul Tannery, eds. Paris: Vrin, 1957-68.

Doubrovsky, Serge. "L'Arrivée de Junie dans *Britannicus:* La Tragédie d'une scène à l'autre." *Littérature* 32 (déc. 1978), pp. 27-54.

——————. *Corneille et la dialectique du héros*. Paris: Gallimard, 1963.

——————. "Corneille: masculin/féminin: Réflexions sur la structure tragique." In *Actes de Tuscon,* Jean-Jacques Demorest and Lise Leibacher-Ouvrard, eds. Paris: Biblio 17, 1984, pp. 89-121.

Dufrenoy, Marie Louise. *L'Orient romanesque en France*. 2 vols. Montréal: Beauchemin, 1946-47.

Ekstein, Nina C. *Dramatic Narrative: Racine's Récits*. New York: Peter Lang, 1986.

Felman, Shoshana. *Le Scandale du corps parlant: Don Juan avec Austin ou La Séduction en deux langues*. Paris: Seuil, 1980.

Foucault, Michel. *L'Archéologie du savoir*. Paris: Gallimard, 1969.

——————. *Histoire de la folie à l'âge classique*. Paris: Gallimard, 1972.

——————. *Les Mots et les choses: Une Archéologie des sciences humaines*. Paris: Gallimard, 1966.

Freud, Sigmund. *The Standard Edition of the Complete Psychological Works of Sigmund Freud*. 24 vols. James Strachey, ed.; James Strachey, Anna Freud, Alix Strachey, and Alan Tyson, trans. London: Hogarth Press, 1953-74.

Genette, Gérard. *Figures II*. Paris: Seuil, 1969.

—————. *Figures III*. Paris: Seuil, 1972.

Girard, René. *Des Choses cachées depuis la fondation du monde*. Paris: Grasset, 1978.

—————. *La Violence et le sacré*. Paris: Grasset, 1972.

Goldmann, Lucien. *Le Dieu caché: Etude sur la vision tragique dans les "Pensées" de Pascal et dans le théâtre de Racine*. Paris: Gallimard, 1959.

—————. *Situation de la critique racinienne*. Paris: l'Arche, 1971.

Goodkin, Richard. "A Choice of Andromache's." In *Concepts of Closure,* David F. Hult, ed., pp. 225-47.

Greenberg, Mitchell. *Corneille, Classicism & The Ruses of Symmetry*. Cambridge: Cambridge University Press, 1987.

—————. *Detours of Desire: Readings in the French Baroque*. Columbus: Ohio State University Press, 1984.

Guy, Basil. *The French Image of China Before and After Voltaire*. Geneva: Droz, 1963.

Hult, David. F., ed. *Concepts of Closure. Yale French Studies* (67), 1984.

Irigaray, Luce. *Speculum de l'autre femme*. Paris: Minuit, 1974.

Jardine, Alice A. Gynesis: *Configurations of Woman and Modernity*. Ithaca: Cornell University Press, 1985.

Judovitz, Dalia. "Autobiographical Discourse and Critical Praxis in Descartes." *Philosophy and Literature* 5 (Spring 1981), pp. 91-107.

—————. *Subjectivity and Representation: The Origins of Modern Thought in Descartes*. Cambridge: Cambridge University Press, 1987.

Kantorowicz, Ernst. *The King's Two Bodies: A Study in Mediaeval Theology*. Princeton: Princeton University Press, 1957.

Kofman, Sarah. *L'Enigme de la femme: La Femme dans les textes de Freud*. Paris: Editions Galilée, 1980.

Kristeva, Julia. *Pouvoirs de l'horreur: Essai sur l'abjection*. Paris: Seuil, 1980.

Kuhn, Reinhard. "The Palace of Broken Words: Reflexions on Racine's *Andromaque.*" *Romanic Review* LXX, 4 (Nov. 1979), pp. 336-45.

Lacan, Jacques. *Ecrits*. Paris: Seuil, 1966.

Lubac, Henri de. *Corpus mysticum: l'Eucharistie et l'église au moyen age*. Paris: Aubier, 1949.

Lyons, John D. "Subjectivity and Imitation in the *Discours de la méthode.*" *Neophilologus* 66 (1982), pp. 508-24.

—————. *A Theatre of Disguise: Studies in French Baroque Drama (1630-1660)*. Columbia, South Carolina: French Literature Publications Company (Summa Publications), 1978.

Lyons, John D. and Nichols, Stephen G., Jr., eds. *Mimesis: From Mirror to Method, Augustine to Descartes*. Hanover: University Press of New England, 1982.

Marin, Louis. *La Critique du discours*. Paris: Minuit, 1975.

—————. *Le Portrait du roi*. Paris: Minuit, 1981.

Martino, Pierre. *L'Orient dans la littérature française au XVIIè et au XVIIIè siècle*. Paris: Librairie Hachette, 1906.

Mauron, Charles. *L'Inconscient dans l'œuvre et la vie de Racine*. Paris: Corti, 1969.

—————. *Phèdre*. Paris: Corti, 1968.

Miller, Nancy K. "Emphasis Added: Plots and Plausibilities in Women's Fiction." *PMLA* 96 (Jan. 1981), pp. 36-48.

Nadal, Octave. *Le Sentiment de l'amour dans l'œuvre de Pierre Corneille.* Paris: Gallimard, 1948.

Nancy, Jean-Luc. *Ego sum*. Paris: Aubier Flammarion, 1979.

Orlando, Francesco. *Towards a Freudian Theory of Literature: With an Analysis of Racine's "Phèdre."* Charmaine Lee, trans. Baltimore: Johns Hopkins University Press, 1978.

Pascal, Blaise. *Pensées*. Paris: Garnier Frères, 1964, ed. Brunschvicg; Intégrale, 1963, ed. Lafuma.

Poulet, Georges. *Les Métamorphoses du cercle*. Paris: Plon, 1961.

Racine, Jean. *Œuvres complètes*. Paris: Seuil, coll. Intégrale, 1962.

Reiss, Timothy J. *The Discourse of Modernism*. Ithaca: Cornell University Press, 1982.

—————. *Tragedy and Truth: Studies in the Development of a Renaissance and Neoclassical Discourse*. New Haven: Yale University Press, 1980.

Rousset, Jean. *Forme et signification: Essais sur les structures littéraires de Corneille à Claudel*. Paris: Corti, 1961; rpt. 1979.

Rycaut, Sir Paul. *Histoire de l'empire ottoman*. Amsterdam: David Mortier, 1714.

Said, Edward W. *Orientalism*. New York: Vintage Books, 1979.

Scherer, Jacques. *Racine et/ou la cérémonie*. Paris: P. U. F., 1982.

—————. *Le Théâtre de Corneille*. Paris: Nizet, 1984.

Siebers, Tobin. *The Mirror of Medusa*. Berkeley: University of California Press, 1983.

Spitzer, Leo. *Etudes de style*. E. Kaufholtz, A. Coulon, M. Foucault, trans. Paris: Gallimard, 1980.

Stegmann, André. *L'Héroïsme cornélien*. 2 vols. Paris: Colin, 1968.

Stiker, Henri-Jacques. "Le Mode de penser de R. Girard." *Esprit* (avril 1979), pp. 46-55.

Stone, Harriet. "Psychic Mechanisms and Heroic Imperatives in *Rodogune, Héraclius,* and *Œdipe.*" *Essays in Literature* 10 (Fall 1983), pp. 283-98.

Woshinsky, Barbara, "Rhetorical Vision in *Le Cid.*" *French Forum* IV, 2 (May 1979), pp. 147-59.

Zimmermann, Eléonore M. "Au delà d'*Athalie.*" *French Forum* V, 1 (Jan. 1980), pp. 14-21.

Index